The
CAT
Who Had
Two Lives

The
CAT
Who Had
Two Lives

BY

Sally Huxley

DONALD I. FINE INC.
New York

Library of Congress Catalogue Card Number: 93-72579

ISBN: 1-55611-386-2

Manufactured in the United States of America

10   9   8   7   6   5   4   3   2   1

DESIGN: Stanley S. Drate/Folio Graphics Co. Inc.

For Pip, Bob, and my parents with love.

*And with gratitude to Hayes Jacobs
and Donald I. Fine, Inc.
who both had faith in a cat.*

CHAPTER *1*

THE CAT WHO CAME IN
FROM THE COLD

*P*ip came to us in the fall. Emaciated, weary, he moved slowly through our fields of dying grass toward the hemlocks along our driveway. The men who were painting our house told us it was as if he were a lost cat returning home. They fed him the remains of a peanut butter sandwich, and as they left, they watched him crawl up the steps onto our porch.

My husband and I had come in late after the painters had finished for the day, and we did not see Pip sleeping on our porch. Though we had moved from New York three months earlier, we still kept an apartment in the city. It was a transitional time for us. Bob worked in the city, and our routine was for him to drive in on Monday and return on Friday. This particular week I had joined him in the city.

My first sight of Pip was through the kitchen window. I was doing the breakfast dishes, working in

1

slow motion. In a new home there were many things to be done far more onerous than washing a plate.

Bob, being a practical man, had already made a list for each of us. Neither included finding a cat that was to be so important in our lives.

"Have you ever seen that cat?" Bob asked, coming up beside me and looking out the window.

"Probably our neighbor's," I said. "White, black patch. Like the pirate in *Treasure Island.*"

"I don't think so," he said. "This one looks sick."

He went outside to investigate while I tried to get a better view. As he walked up the stairs on the porch, Pip crawled out from under a wagon I had filled with pumpkins for Halloween. He was thin, scruffy, and he moved slowly, warily, hiding behind gourds and a stalk of corn tied to the railings, before he rested his head on Bob's shoes. Pip's ribs showed through the fur. What I remember most was the intense yellow of his eyes.

From the moment I saw him up close, I felt bonded to him in some undefinable way. I had grown up in a small town, and had decided that as soon as I was old enough I would leave. College had been the first of many steps that would take me away. Marriage had been the last and permanent step.

I remembered asking the town clerk for a form to change my surname on my Pennsylvania drivers license after I was married. I told her that I would eventually get a New York license.

She looked at me and said that there wasn't any

reason to bother, because she knew I was coming back.

"And what if I were stopped in New York?" I asked.

"Nobody'd believe that you wanted to live there all your life."

I resisted telling her that I had been plotting my departure from Emlenton from the time I was a teenager. Ironically, I always kept my Pennsylvania drivers license, by using my parents' address.

From the beginning Pip was my link to the house, to a way of life that I thought I had wisely abandoned.

I stood on the porch beside Pip. He looked up and tried to purr. Not knowing what to do, I went inside and fixed scrambled eggs. I'm certain that somewhere in my Presbyterian upbringing, scrambled eggs were akin to chicken soup. Pip was starved. Even though Bob and I were cat apprentices, we knew enough to feed him small meals, often, because his stomach was shrunken from months of deprivation. He lifted his head up from the plate and rubbed against me.

"He likes your eggs. You put half-and-half in them?" Bob asked.

I nodded. Culinary habits were hard to break.

We decided that unless I modified Pip's diet, he would end up with high cholesterol. I went to the supermarket for cat food. I never expected to see anything remotely connected to a cat on my shopping list, yet alone at the top and underlined.

I was surprised that for someone who still ate

bacon with nitrates and mayonnaise with real yolks I was reading all the labels on the cat food cans. I was certain that our cat—already I was thinking in terms of our cat—would prefer small cans with discreet labeling, not any Madison Avenue hype: Morris and Nine Lives, or the nameless, smug feline on Kal Kan.

We never considered a cat to be a pet. We had friends in the city who had cats, and always said when they moved to a larger apartment or out of New York, they would get a dog. We thought of cats as substitute pets, understudies for the role of the real pet.

My sister told me that there had been a cat in our family before I was born. She referred to Tabby in much the same way as someone refers to an eccentric relative. Tabby apparently only ate on the roof of our house. To make feeding him easier, Dad left the ladder up, so it looked as if someone were always in the process of eloping. Aside from that cat and an alligator my uncle had sent my sister from South America, when the postal service accepted packages with air holes in them, my family had had only dogs. Eduardo, the gator, lived in the downstairs bathtub. Mysteriously, whenever my mother's bridge club met, he escaped, slithering into the living room, and nipped their ankles. I can still hear my mother saying, "All right. Who let the alligator out?" Eduardo eventually was given to a zoo.

Except for the brief lapse with Eduardo and the roof cat, our family's dog owning record was unbroken.

Considering Eduardo, it seemed strange that I would think of a cat as an odd choice for a pet, but I believed all the propaganda about them. Cats were not affectionate, they ripped the upholstery off furniture, they were sneaky and cunning, but then I looked at Pip and wondered if I had been wrong.

After I unloaded the three bags of cat food, I decided Pip needed medical care, so I looked for the name and number of the veterinarian who'd been recommended. I called Dr. Tindall and told him about Pip. Actually, at that time we called him Annie.

"A stray," I said. "Thin. Hair falling out."

"How long has the cat been there?"

"About two hours," I said.

"Don't you think you should wait and see if it stays?"

"No," I said. I was firm about that. The cat needed medical care.

Bob and I waited, uncertain what to expect. All we had been told about Dr. Tindall was that he was good and made housecalls. Although I did not expect him to be driving a sports car, I was surprised when he arrived in a van about the size of our front porch. His hospital on wheels, I later learned, had an operating room for emergency and routine surgery. Clad in jeans and a denim vest, Dr. Tindall was a sort of Country Western vet who believed in treating animals on their home turf where they were more comfortable. He pronounced Annie a he, a neutered male, about two years old, obviously someone's housecat that had been turned out. He said that unless we wanted to add to Pip's problems by giving him a gender crisis we should rename him.

"Annie was only a working title," we said. Until now, I thought that people who didn't know the sex of animals had had a puritanical upbringing and never bothered to look. Not knowing she was a he seemed to typecast us as foolish New Yorkers.

Dr. Tindall said that Pip was on the verge of starvation and had a week or two left at most. "But he's a fighter," he said. "And he has enough pride left to still groom."

Dr. Tindall told us we were Pip's last hope. I prefer to think that he was destined to come to us, that he just had a difficult time finding the address, something I shared in common with him. After we bought the house of our dreams, I drove by it twice when I was to meet the real estate agent who sold it to us.

All four of us—Bob, Doc, the now renamed Pip, and I sat on various levels of the porch steps. It was a spur-of-the-moment name. If Bob had read *A Tale of Two Cities*, instead of *Great Expectations*, Pip might have been given a far, far better name. At least, name to the contrary, he was no longer an orphan boy.

All we needed were grandpa and grandma in rocking chairs to complete a Norman Rockwell painting. Pip, of course, would have to be touched up. He had lost most of the fur on the right side of his face from an infected puncture wound, probably inflicted by another cat.

Everything was harmonious until Dr. Tindall took out several vials of serum. I have always judged a doctor's skills by his ability to run. Our old family physician had to chase my middle sister around the house twice to vaccinate her for polio. By the time I came along, his medical knowledge had waned, and his jogging days were over. Just as Pip started to run, Tindall jumped up, grabbed him, and gave him his shots. I knew by the speed at which he moved that we had the family vet.

The steroid shot to build up Pip's body weight increased his appetite to such an extent that he was soon eating six meals a day on the porch. In addition, I gave him treats that smelled of fish.

"Maybe we'll let him in the kitchen," we said to Dr. Tindall when he came back to give Pip his second round of vaccinations. I was holding Pip by the collar because he had recognized the van and started to run. Cats, it seemed, remembered. Tindall said that he could inoculate a dog and a minute later it would lick his face, while a cat looked at him as if it were trying to fix his face in its memory for retribution.

"About the kitchen," Tindall said, "remember he's a cat. Let him in all of your house, or keep him outside. He won't be satisfied with only one room."

We listened. Having owned a cat for less than a month, we thought we were experts. Even then we were wrong. You never completely own a cat.

Bob and I never thought about letting Pip in the house. We were still influenced by years of misinformation. The farmer down the road had over a dozen barn cats that seemed content. If our barn had been roomy enough for horses, certainly it would accommodate a small cat. If Pip had been outside this long and survived, he knew how to take care of himself. We would provide shelter—the barn—and food and medical care.

The woman who owned the house before us had two cats that she named after characters in *Gone With the Wind*. Pitty Pat and Butler were opposites. We had a brush with Butler one day. He hissed and snarled and sat on the kitchen table daring us, it seemed, to buy the house and displace him. We made certain he didn't come with the house.

The other problem, aside from damaged furniture, was the litter box. This woman had used one of the upstairs bathtubs to hold the litter in a plastic box. It so happened that Butler had just been in there a moment before we looked.

The idea of a cat in residence seemed so remote that we referred to the room as the dirty little bathroom and made plans to replace the bathtub.

We proceeded to convert the barn into a bedroom for Pip. We bought bales of straw. Straw, we were told, would make a better mattress than hay, which was only grass clippings. Bob was intent on finding the right stuff for the mattress. Before we were married he insisted that I lie down on several mattresses in Altman's and give them a test sleep. I was embarrassed then. This time Bob tested the firmness by sitting on the bale.

The country was starting to come back to me. I remembered hay rides, or were they straw rides, that I would sneeze my way through. I hoped that Pip did not have a similar allergic reaction. He did, however, have a reaction. He wanted nothing to do with the barn.

I had Bob rearrange the bales one more time and spread some of the straw on the boards. It looked perfect. The only thing missing was a cat.

"It'll take time," Bob said.

Pip decided to sleep in our carriage house. The upper part was now an apartment and the lower half a garage. At least it was a room with a view, a view of our house. We moved the cars outside to give Pip a larger apartment.

Often when I saw Pip sitting in one of his sphinx-like poses, I thought that he was not contemplating his name, as T. S. Eliot suggested, but a way to break into our house.

Our resolve was beginning to weaken every time we saw Pip shivering and looking with absolute disgust at the straw manger scene we had created. I bought Pip a round, quilted bed with a hood. He looked like an oracle in his hut, all eyes, staring out, making silent pronouncements.

We cut a hole in the garage door to allow him to go in and out at will. He seemed to like the idea of not having a curfew. We covered the hole in the garage with thin plastic strips that could be easily pushed aside. Coaxing Pip from his igloo, we demonstrated how easy it was to go in and out any time he wanted.

"Now you try it," Bob said. He looked at Pip, and Pip looked at me. I felt obligated to do something constructive.

I pointed to the door.

Pip looked as if I had just told him his door was the servants' entrance. There was nothing else to do. I picked him up and tried to put his head through the opening. Spread-eagled, he dug his claws into the wood. Then he jumped down and licked his paws.

I was not about to grovel in front of a cat, and unless we cut the hole extra, extra large, I couldn't put anything except my hand through the opening to demonstrate. What we needed was the Artful Dodger. While we revised our strategy, Pip batted the strips and went outside.

The first winter we had Pip the weather was harsh with high winds and drifting snow. As we shoveled the snow from his door, he'd push one paw out and then draw it back quickly. I was afraid he was going to freeze.

I found myself going outside in the cold more than I ordinarily would have. Like Pip, I liked warmth. I'd bundle up and under the pretense of going for a walk, I'd make certain Pip was all right.

Bob still went into the city, but I found less and less reason to go with him. Now I was making excuses to

stay in the country. I needed to clean the house. I needed
to kill the crabgrass. Bob's rival was Pip.

On frigid days Pip stayed in his igloo, his yellow eyes
staring out, staring through us. He wouldn't come out to
eat. I eventually held his dish for him, so all he had to do
was stick his head out.

It was then we decided to get the kerosene heater.
We read Consumer Reports and bought the brand the
magazine recommended.

"You know about K-2, don't you?" the station owner
asked.

"You mean the mountain?"

He looked puzzled for a moment, then said, "No, I'm
talking kerosene. K-2's the bad stuff. I only sell K-1,
good way to heat if you do it proper," he continued. "No
substitute. Good ventilation, and it'll keep you safe and
warm. I don't care what these city people tell you."

We didn't tell him it was for our cat.

The garage had adequate ventilation. Though stur-
dily built, it was over a hundred years old and had gaps
between the boards.

We lighted the heater and the "white lightning" did
not smoke. We settled into a routine. Heater lighted at
night, and turned off in the morning.

I was worried about fire and checked on Pip. Sometimes I disturbed his sleep. Though Pip could sleep
through almost anything, he showed his displeasure at
my tiptoeing. I sometimes felt as if I were a mother
looking in on her child, rejoicing that the baby was

sleeping through the night, then frantically wondering why. Bob suggested I get an intercom.

I was in charge of buying the kerosene. I knew which stations sold the real stuff. I felt as if I were trafficking in something illegal, going from place to place asking about the purity of the kerosene.

I became a regular customer at Mr. Bly's, the station owner who first told me about K-1. I routinely hoisted the ten-gallon can into the back of the station wagon, while Mr. Bly remarked about how strong women were these days, that it wasn't like old times.

One day a young boy—I remember he was wearing a baseball cap and a jacket with a horseshoe on the back—reached for the can. If I had still been in New York, I would have held onto it, thinking he had an ulterior motive. Instead I smiled, and he lifted the can into the car.

The shortest way back to our house was over narrow country roads with hairpin curves. I was driving the station wagon slowly and was almost to the railroad crossing perched on a hill, when a truck came straight at me. I moved off the road, hitting the edge of the tracks. The truck kept going. As I pulled off, I heard a sound best described as a cannonball rolling.

I stopped farther up the road and opened the door. The kerosene can was on its side in the back of the wagon. The boy had forgotten to put the cap on, and kerosene was rolling slowly toward the front seat. I opened all the windows and froze the rest of the way home. Pip was waiting in front of the carriage house for his fuel delivery.

He seemed to enjoy watching me try to clean the carpet in the car. I poured charcoal in the back and then emptied my second best bottle of perfume. The only thing that accomplished was to make me sneeze.

I called the station and was told that they were pumpers, not lifters. To add insult to injury Mr. Bly, who had always called me by my first name, said, "Mrs. Huxley, this area is just getting too crowded for me with all these city people moving in." He also said he'd thrown out the cap to my kerosene container.

I wanted to tell him a city person would have been wary of anyone nice and checked the can before closing the car door.

I phoned the insurance company two days later. Honesty was the best policy, and speaking of policy, I wasn't certain I was covered. I already knew from talking to the repair shop that all the carpeting and the back seat needed to be replaced to get rid of the overpowering smell.

"Unusual," our representative said. "But it's covered under accident. It was an accident?"

"Of course." I tried to sound indignant, but I knew I was in no position to sound anything other than dumb.

"And what were you doing with the kerosene?" I could hear her pen writing.

"It was for the heater for my cat." I was losing

credibility fast, but at least she didn't think I hated animals.

The insurance agent lived in the town where I grew up. My parents had used her company. Despite her insistence that she would handle the matter discreetly, I knew that somehow the story would filter out. I may have physically left the town, but the anecdotes lingered on.

"Kerosene, doesn't that girl know better?" And everyone in the town would probably say No.

Later we bought an electric heater made in Italy. A foreign heater was an improvement over domestic kerosene. Nothing but the best for our barn cat. Pip was fortunate that he didn't have to worry about anyone's balance of payments other than Bob's and mine.

Since Bob commuted on a weekly basis, Pip was my companion during the week. When he heard the door open, he ran from wherever he was and joined me. He would purr and rub against me, giving me his "I'm so little trouble" routine.

I have always been a pushover for animals. I didn't see any harm in letting him into the kitchen. I could shut the door, so I did. He seemed content to explore. He sat in cupboards and jumped on the window ledge, maneuvering between the houseplants.

Sure, there was white hair caught on the crown of thorns and a clump of fur I couldn't explain in the cupboard with canned vegetables—Pip had been grooming. Bob did notice, however, that I was always wiping up the counter. Housecleaning had always been low on my list of priorities.

I told Bob I was getting gray. I expected him to disagree. Instead, he asked me what I was doing with my head in a plant.

I suppose Bob knew that I was letting Pip inside, but he was afraid to ask. I could almost envision a scene with Bob saying, "Me or the cat?" More and more I wanted to be with Pip. I enjoyed having him around me, and I began referring to him as my little boy. I always thought that was silly before. I reassured myself that I still had some sense left because I wasn't calling him my son.

I began to think of Bob's and my life together. I had never imagined that we would be married over a decade and have no children. Being of the generation that could choose, I had put off the decision of having children. Always next year, I'd say, like some battle cry. Pip filled the void.

In the cooler months, when there was a fire in the fireplace, I carried Pip from the kitchen to the den. It seems silly now, but I think my reasoning was that if his paws never touched the floor he wouldn't remember where he'd been. Pip was no doubt making detailed mental blueprints.

At first he was afraid of the fire and hid underneath a chair, but eventually, Pip liked the fire as much as I did. I told him that his visits were our secret.

Bob was logical; an outdoor cat belonged outdoors.

"Even when he's allergic?" I said.

Pip did have allergies to spring pollens, and sneezed with great alacrity when Bob was around. Tindall said we could give Pip a pill every day, but I realized if I started all that, I would be in some home, crocheting antimacassars and trying to remember what they were. Pip was not a cat that took his medicine lying down.

I also was beginning to realize that I was sneezing more, nose running, and for the first time in years my asthma was bothering me. I tried to figure out the change—the country with all its pollen. Even though I knew better, I refused to acknowledge that the main allergen was rubbing up against me, becoming more and more important in my life. If it came to it, Pip and I would just take our medicine together.

By May Bob was spending most weekends in his well-organized garden. I have always maintained broccoli didn't care what it was next to, or even if it was in a wobbly run, but Bob planted his crops with military procession. Pip helped, by digging some holes and fertilizing them. He weeded the catnip planted by the previous owner.

Bob still had an aversion to the smell of litter.

I assured him that I could find a container smaller and neater than a tub and that I would change the litter daily. I remembered begging my parents for a dog—"I'll feed it. Promise, promise." Dad later said that if our dog depended on me for food, we would have the only three-pound dog in captivity.

In summer Pip ate meals with us on the terrace.

Bob delighted in telling people that Pip was an outdoor cat, that he would never be allowed inside. Our cat-owning friends smiled, and kept their thoughts to themselves.

Like Henry Higgins, Bob was grooming Pip. In no time he would have this cat shaped up, or was it the other way around?

Pip finally came in from the cold in the fall. I do not remember the day. I like to think there was this great epiphany, but now I cannot remember which one of us opened the door. It was a turning point, and Pip became an even greater presence in our lives.

We would look at the counter where he was grooming and then look away for a moment. He would be gone, as if he were a sprite vanishing into the air, never letting us possess him. When I tried to hold him, he would squirm. Whenever we opened a door, he would try to go outside.

Bob would shake his head. "We let him in, and now he wants to go outside. Isn't that just like a cat?"

"Just like a cat," I repeated, and for the first time I had the feeling that I would never understand what that meant.

From the moment he came inside, I thought of him as an indoor cat and under my protection. Considering the months he had been on his own, or the times I had watched him in the yard chasing a falling leaf, or sitting at the edge of the field waiting for mice, it seemed silly that it was only when he came inside that I began to fear

The cat who came in from the cold.

the outdoors for him, that I began to wonder what his life before us had been. I wanted a history for Pip. It was almost as if I knew that lacking a past, I would try to make up for all the wrongs, imagined or real.

CHAPTER 2

ARTHUR THE BLACK KNIGHT

*A*rthur lived next door. He was a thug, a bully, a street-smart cat with one cocked ear. He was the feline version of a boxer, who'd taken one too many punches but was still around on his feet, waiting to take on newcomers.

The first time I saw Arthur he was hanging from the screen door in our kitchen. He was resting batlike, pressing his already flat nose against the screen. Bob and I had moved into our house the previous week. Even though I was certain that Arthur was not the welcome wagon, I wondered if he might be some primitive initiation into country life.

When Arthur didn't move, I began to think he was stuck to the door and that he would become a permanent decoration, appropriate only at Halloween. He retracted his claws when I brought him food. I put down a bowl of milk, which he lapped up, leaving white residue not only on his cheeks, but his paws as well. He looked up at me as if he expected a main course with his beverage.

Arthur was a likeable cat, sociable, affectionate. He was lumplike, a clump of black fur with bushy cheeks that stood out at almost the same angle as his whiskers. He was built too low to the ground to produce the type of swagger he seemed to intend when he walked.

Like most cats, Arthur didn't recognize property lines. Even after Bob and I arrived, he seemed to believe in the right of adverse possession. He napped in our barn and fished in our pond.

We own twenty acres, and Arthur's family — a sea captain, his wife and three dogs, including a cat-hating rottweiler that Arthur set straight by cuffing her on her nose — have the eighty acres that surround us in a horseshoe shape. Arthur belongs to the landed gentry, although in the hierarchy of cats, his birth would have been in the stables and not talked about in the manor house.

Arthur looked upon us as squatters.

He languished on our terrace in the late afternoon. He did his best to look emaciated, and worthy of a handout. He ate snacks from our hands, even when the snacks were intended for us and not him. He preferred Jalapeño Fritos.

In the summer we ate dinner on the terrace. One night, Arthur announced himself, as he usually did, with a great deal of fanfare and clumsiness. Cats measure the distance they want to jump by looking and calculating. Arthur had the same problem as the Wright Brothers: how to lift a heavy cargo. He glanced once, then jumped. When he landed on a plate, instead of the table, it didn't seem to matter. At least he had been airborne. As he stretched, he knocked over a wine glass. While we swept up the shards and tried to keep Arthur from getting glass in the pads of his feet, he was, as they say, otherwise engaged. We had left food on the table and since *we* weren't eating it . . .

Everything we had ever heard about the graceful feline turned out to be myth in Arthur's case. He lumbered, he stomped, he crashed into things, but never once did he walk on "little cat feet."

As long as we were catless, Arthur was content. As with most cats, he preferred the status quo, and the status quo did not include Pip. Arthur formed an instant and permanent dislike for Pip. At first we tried to mediate, to tell them that there was no reason why two cats could not get along, especially if one stayed on his own property.

The problem was that Arthur was a tomcat, an unneutered male with hormones intact, and he immediately established his dominance over Pip. We felt rather like the parents of a child who is roughed up each day by the town bully. While we wanted to teach Pip the principles of nonagression, we also wanted to pummel Arthur ourselves.

As long as Arthur confined his activities to hissing,

that was okay. I felt terrible that Pip cowered, while Arthur began marking out his fiefdom on Pip's property. He wet on all the terrace plants. He ate his prey on our porch, in front of Pip, who crouched low to the ground, his tail underneath him. Arthur was determined to run Pip out of town.

Arthur hung out in our pachysandra, waiting to mug Pip. He clumped through it, rustling the leaves whenever he began one of his attacks on Pip. Arthur's idea of a sneak attack was a frontal assault. Pip always knew he was coming, and that might have been part of Arthur's MO.

Arthur, the Black Knight, begins his version of a frontal assault.

Pip was no match for Arthur, and he would have been hurt more often if Arthur had not been a klutz.

It seemed as if the world of my childhood was in front of me. Arthur was the black knight, Mordred, and Pip was Lancelot the pure. Since Pip was neutered there would be no feline Guinevere to blur the lines between good and evil.

Bob and I liked Arthur, which was part of the problem. Although we had known him longer than Pip, Pip was our cat, and we felt somewhat disloyal by allowing Arthur to sit on the terrace. We tried to ignore him. We figured that with subtle hints Arthur would get the point, but one could never be subtle with Arthur. Spell it out for him and he couldn't get past the first letter. He would sit and look at us, waiting for further clarification.

I had heard stories about male cats fighting. I was determined that if the fur were to fly it would be Arthur's and not Pip's.

We eventually decided we should chase Arthur away.

"What about a gun?" Bob said. He was reading an article on altering cat behavior.

"Sounds pretty drastic," I said. "That would really alter him."

"It says if you add a little ammonia to the water."

It was then I realized he was talking about a squirt gun.

We bought a squirt gun and filled it with water,

then added a drop of ammonia. Even though Arthur was a big enough target, I decided that Bob would be the better gunslinger.

We didn't have to wait for high noon or anything so symbolic. Arthur slunk onto our porch the day after we bought the squirt gun. He purred and rubbed up against us, hissed at Pip, and raised his paw.

Bob drew his gun and squirted him on the middle of his back, avoiding his eyes. Arthur looked up to see if it was raining, then went back to tormenting Pip.

"Go home, Arthur," we said.

Arthur finally obliged us a couple of hours later when he decided we were not going to feed him.

We read other articles, which were just as helpful—throw water on a cat to dampen its "ardor." Obviously Arthur's intentions were not amorous, but the article assured us that almost all cats hate water and the sensation of being wet.

Once when my sister was visiting, Arthur began to attack Pip, and she threw a full glass of water at him. Arthur sat down in the puddle and groomed. Was he perhaps Scotchguarded?

Pip and Arthur's feuding continued over the months, with occasional truces declared that were eventually broken, then renegotiated. Pip was always giving up something.

We still separated them physically. They were like children making faces at each other. I'd pick Pip up, and carry him inside, while Arthur skulked around the outside with Bob giving him some friendly advice.

Because Pip's fur was mostly white, we could tell if he'd been in a fight.

Arthur struck often and at all hours. Each cat has a certain voice, a way of communicating, and we began to recognize Pip's various meows and cries.

I soon learned that a pucture wound and not a scratch caused problems. Cats have the ability to heal almost immediately, and the skin closes over a puncture. Bacteria from the claws stay inside and can cause infection.

In truth, I was frightened. Arthur's attacks were increasing, and despite his ineptitude, he was inflicting more damage on Pip. I spent most of my day shadowing Pip, feeling much like a mother who sends her child off on a bicycle and then watches from the bushes.

Whenever I heard Pip cry, I would run.

My father-in-law once remarked that the reason Bob and I did not have any children was because of that "damned cat." I laughed at him, but in an odd way he was right. Pip was my substitute baby. He needed me not only to provide food but to protect him. If I didn't see Pip—being white, he was easy to spot except in the snow—I would go outside and hang around on the terrace hoping he would see me loitering and come from wherever he was.

It is hard to believe that one hot fall night, before Pip was allowed into the house, I heard him screech and hiss

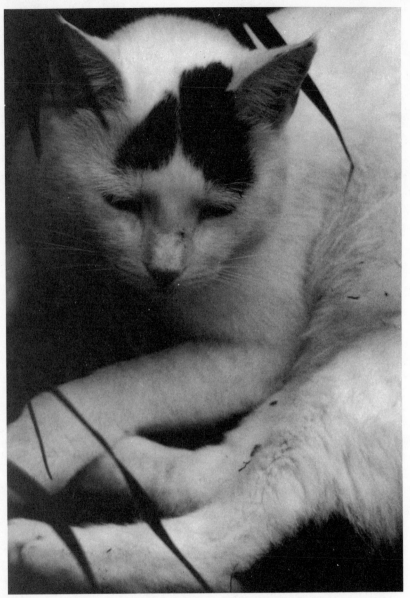

Arthur landed a right cross directly on Pip's nose.

through the open bedroom window. I tried to sleep, but the sounds were so intense, I knew there was another animal out there, probably a raccoon. I waited until the noise stopped. I wasn't about to go outside and see a wounded cat. I remember thinking that at least it was quick.

When I finally went outside, Pip was on the terrace. He was unhurt but scared, and I was ashamed. I bent down and called him over. He rubbed against my leg, while I sat down on the flagstone and cried. From then on, I overreacted to his travails with Arthur. I suppose I was always trying to make amends for failing him.

One day while Pip was sleeping, Arthur attacked. I had called Dr. Tindall twice before on similar occasions. By now he not only knew my voice but anticipated what I was going to say.

"It's that Arthur again." If his answering machine was on, I left incriminating messages. "It was Arthur again. I could kill him. He hurt Pip."

Pip's medical file was thicker than ours. Each time Dr. Tindall came to see Pip he gave him a shot to prevent any infection.

"Have you considered neutering Arthur?" Dr. Tindall said on his fifth visit.

"He's not ours," I said, "and I couldn't ask our neighbors." I was ready to wound Arthur's pride, but I could not bring myself to harm his body.

"You could tell me he's your cat. I'll believe you." He was kidding, of course, and when he saw we were mulling over his offer, he said he didn't mean it.

I decided that I was being overprotective, turning Pip into a mama's boy. After all, he had existed for two years without his bodyguards.

The next time Arthur struck I decided I would wait and not panic. I could monitor Pip's health. I knew the warning signs. If he didn't eat . . . hardly likely, I thought. If he didn't groom . . . When I finally called Dr. Tindall thirty-six hours later, Pip had developed an abscess, a sore near the back of his legs that was red and tender. Arthur apparently had caught him fleeing and had jabbed him with his claw; hardly good sportsmanship, I thought. If I had waited any longer, Pip would have had to have surgery. Pip was almost too weak to run from Dr. Tindall as he usually did, but he did try to limp away.

The area near his tail was inflamed. Dr. Tindall cut away some hair, which gave Pip an odd male pattern baldness. He gave Pip an antibiotic and told us to apply salve to the wound three times a day. In addition we were to administer a pill each morning and night for a week.

Bob and I looked at each other. We thought we could handle that. We nodded. Then Dr. Tindall gave us a bottle of pills.

"Two a day," he said.

We nodded. Surely we could manage to give a pill to a ten-pound cat. If we couldn't reason, we could gang up on him and apply brute force.

The good doctor explained how to pill a cat. I wasn't

certain if it was a verb or not, but it sounded correct. To pill or not. I preferred the negative version.

We listened intently and tried not to look either baffled or stupid.

Yes, we understood.

After Dr. Tindall left, I looked at Bob and said, "I don't understand."

We decided that acting confident was the best approach. We smiled at Pip and tried to open the adult-proof pill bottle. We were not inspiring confidence in him. It took us five minutes to get the cap off. He was still watching us. He looked as if I were about to chloroform him. I had about as much chance of giving him a pill as Arthur did.

Bob and I worked in tandem. Two reasonably smart adults were not going to be outwitted by a cat. Bob opened Pip's mouth, pulled his lip back over his teeth, which looked menacingly sharp, while I tossed the pill. It was like trying to make a basket when you were the shortest person on the team. I blew on his nose, as Bob did, and together we created a gale force. We waited for the natural reflex to swallow that Tindall had mentioned. Pip's natural reaction was to spit the pill out beneath a table. One of us then had to crawl under the table to retrieve the pill. Obviously, this was some form of penitence.

"Here, Pip," I said. I was about to say that this was for his own good, when Bob grabbed me by the hand and shook his head.

"Never con a cat," he said.

We reversed roles. I held Pip while Bob tossed the pill, equally unsuccessfully. Pip was still playing the role of an unwilling cat.

I knew we would have to change our tactics or there wouldn't be enough hours in a day to give Pip two pills. I eventually mashed up his pills and put them in his favorite food.

Arthur patrolled the perimeter of the house, periodically checking on the patient. It was almost as if he were allowing Pip time to recuperate before he attacked again.

I thought we had arrived at a meaningful truce, albeit tentative. There were minor incursions, but all in all it was holding. The thick band of trees between the houses seemed to be a no-cat's-land.

One evening I called Pip. Usually he was sitting outside the kitchen door, waiting to be coaxed inside to be offered a bedtime snack.

I went outside and called again. No Pip. Every half hour I came downstairs and looked. It was a warm summer night, and Pip's suggested bedtime was later than in the winter months, but under no circumstances was he allowed to stay out all night. There was no negotiating. I was firm about that.

Bob felt that Pip could stay out most of the night, applying the same double standard to male cats as he did to teenage boys. I wanted Pip in bed by ten.

"He's probably chasing a mouse," Bob said the third time I woke him up to tell him that Pip was still outside. I decided to go look for him.

I stood on the terrace and called and whistled. As I was going upstairs I heard a meow, small and tiny, but certainly Pip's. I looked outside and saw Pip in a bed of lilies next to the house. Arthur had backed him up against the wall. Arthur was enjoying himself grooming, although as always he looked disheveled and dusty. Pip stared at me with his yellow eyes, while Arthur flattened himself and hissed.

I decided to do what I did best—I called Bob. Pip pleaded with me, meowing even more as I went inside, leaving him with his nemesis, Arthur the black knight.

I felt terrible leaving Pip, but enough was enough, and if someone had to set Arthur on the path of righteousness, or at least the path to his house, it should be Bob.

"It's Arthur," I yelled at Bob. "He's trapped Pip against the wall." I made it sound as if a firing squad were imminent.

Bob recalls I said that Arthur was hurting my little boy.

Bob ran downstairs au naturel. By now Pip knew that reinforcements had arrived, and he was starting to make his move. Arthur was lethargic. I picked up Pip, who was showing all signs of latent bravery, including teeth.

Pip and I tried to provide the proper encouragement for Bob, who by now felt foolish. I was wearing a robe, and both cats had fur, but Bob was in the buff, standing on the flagstone terrace with Arthur licking his toes.

"Make him go home," I said.

Bob looked at me and shook his head. "Pip doesn't listen. You don't listen. Why should Arthur?" It was difficult to argue with a naked man, especially when he was right.

Bob looked around the terrace. There was a broom propped up against a wooden bench. Bob picked it up and raised it above his head. Arthur stared at him as if he expected Bob to sweep the porch. He didn't move. Even though he'd never seen Bob naked, he still recognized him as a friend. Besides, it was dark and Arthur saw better in the darkness.

Finally Arthur started to move across the terrace. Pip was trying to careen out of my arms, hissing as Arthur slunk by. Bob looked at me, shrugged, and waved the broom.

His cheerleading squad was behind him, shouting encouragement.

Arthur moved slowly, looking back every so often as though he wasn't certain whether Bob was playing a game. Arthur would scurry, then stop, almost as if he were waiting for Bob to pat him.

Arthur looked mystified, and we weren't certain whether the confusion was because someone who was usually friendly was acting unfriendly, or because there was a nude man with a broom running after him, yelling. Being curious and perhaps a little prurient, Arthur kept looking back. I must admit I looked, too. The sight of Bob, running through the yard naked, waving a broom, should have been enough to scare any cat.

Finally, Arthur ran under the wild rose bushes. Bob stopped because the bushes were waist high. I applauded Bob's bravery and his good sense. Then I hurried inside. The air was nippy.

Cats know almost as many ways to annoy each other as humans do. The only time Pip ever challenged Arthur was when I was sitting on the bench on the terrace. Arthur came romping through the pachysandra. He brushed against my leg and then jumped onto my lap. Pip arched his back and came charging out from underneath the bench, hissing, spitting, driving Arthur away. Arthur never looked back.

It was a great day for the white knight.

CHAPTER 3

BASIC TRAINING

As the days went by, we realized that it was no longer our house. Somehow we had deeded it over to Pip, and he was allowing us to live there as tenants because of his extraordinary generosity.

We had a lot to learn about cats, and if we wanted to coexist in *his* house, we would have to shape up. After all we were dog people. Smile at a dog, it smiles. Feed it, it eats. Yell at it, it loves you. Those were the basic tenets of animal behavior as we knew them. Pip was about to enlighten us.

Although we were not naive enough to expect obedience from Pip, we did anticipate a modicum of gratitude and respect, and a friendly purr. Sometimes, though, I felt as if Bob and I were sitting in a half-empty theater, watching an actor audition for one of those confusing Pinter plays. Pip seemed to display the proper emotions of displeasure, disgust, and annoyance in our presence, but he was weak on the more joyful poses.

Initially, we tried to treat him as if he were a

scaled-down version of a dog. Though I have often seen Pip sit on the edge of a field waiting for a blade of grass to move, his patience with us was limited. We began to realize that our behavior was unacceptable.

If we truly annoyed Pip, he would retaliate in his own way. With Bob, he used the direct approach. One morning when Bob was shaving, Pip came into the bathroom and licked his leg. I was relieved that Pip was becoming more affectionate, easier to manage. In actuality, he was disinfecting the skin before he sunk his teeth into Bob's flesh. Retribution accomplished, Pip fled. He didn't seem to be a cat that held grudges long, except where I was concerned.

With me he was more subtle. I have collected dolls since I was a child, and with Pip around my dolls were in jeopardy. If I offended him in any small way, he would exact revenge on my dolls. He would pull off their wigs and shred the hair, and then knock the dolls onto the floor.

Usually, though, if we behaved properly, Pip would consider our request and then get back to us.

If we wanted to have a conversation with Pip, we had to address him directly, without any gestures, and at all times we were to remember that there were no bad cats, only uninformed owners. Since a cat sees things on a horizontal plane, not vertical, it was not only useless but demeaning to point.

Pip liked his meals on demand. One meow was sufficient warning. If I fed him anything that came

Pip had a love-hate relationship with my dolls.

from a large can, he would arch his back, look at his
bowl with great contempt, and walk away for good.
Generic cat food was not in his vocabulary. After all
he was not a generic cat. He made it clear that he did
not like liver—anyone's liver, chicken, cow, or even

mouse. He didn't consider liver to be either a source of protein or a culinary delight.

Even when we didn't ask Pip for an opinion, he gave us one. He was most vocal about his dining arrangements. He wanted both haute cuisine and ambience. He seemed bewildered that we didn't eat our evening meal together. He didn't have to be at the head of the table, but he at least wanted to be at the table, or better yet on it.

Once when an elderly southern aunt was visiting us, Pip jumped on the table next to a leg of lamb. He appeared to be guarding it. "He never does that," we said with the confidence of someone who announces that it never rains in London.

"Don't you all worry," she said. "I never eat lamb."

Pip was content to be a centerpiece until we asked him to get down. Annoyed, he jumped down and went into the living room where I heard two of my dolls hit the floor.

Once, when I had Pip in a conciliatory mood, I decided to tell him my views on begging. "Good cats don't beg," I said. I could tell by the way he looked he was about to offer a rebuttal, but I patted him and called him a "Good cat." I knew he thought I was stating the obvious. Cats accept praise, but they are not overwhelmed by it.

Pip gave every indication he understood. No problem, I thought, as I started to peel the shrimp. He jumped up on the counter to assist me.

"Good cat," I said, hoping to make him listen. "No begging." He was too busy playing with a shrimp to hear me.

I lifted him down, and like any true cat he was back up again, after taking a detour. I set up barriers, mined his way to the shrimp field. He simply took a bumpier, more direct route over the top of the flour canister and ended up at the sink again.

We were about to have our first serious disagreement. "Shrimp is for people," I said. "Not kitty cats."

Having animals reduces one to foolishness. He wasn't buying any of this, and he resented my diction. We both knew that shrimp was more interesting than anything in his dish, but I was firm. I would not be taken advantage of so early on in this relationship.

What I learned was that it is impossible to outstare a cat. It cannot be done. Cats are able to focus on something and then consider it to be their life's occupation. I blinked first. Cats would make perfect spies; you can never break them down. Eventually I weakened and gave him a shrimp. He pushed it toward me, and sat patiently while I peeled it for him.

Pip huffed off after I refused to give him any more shrimp. He had the look of a diner who had ordered a shrimp cocktail and found mostly shredded lettuce. He amused himself on the window ledge, bullying my plants. He decided to take a nap when he realized I was paying no attention to him.

We found out quickly that Pip could ignore loud

noises—a dishwasher, a vacuum cleaner, a Fourth of July celebration—but a whisper or a refrigerator door opening would wake him up. He would have made the perfect watch cat if a burglar intended only to take food.

The first week of our intensive training was the most difficult.

Pip broke me of a lifelong habit of leaving doors open. Once I found him sitting in my spices between the white and cayenne peppers, eating a bay leaf. He could fit inside a pan and curl up, and he believed that boots were made for sleeping, not walking. He was slowly proving to me that in the game of hide-and-seek he would always win.

Little by little he explored the house, forming his own internal maps, charting places we never imagined. Even the familiar took on the mystery of unexplored territory. I had never thought my closets interesting, although potentially lethal, perhaps, because of all the things I had crammed into them, but they amused Pip. Sitting on shelves and contemplating out-of-date clothes became a daily sport. Outside, he found time not only to stop and smell the roses, but to scratch his nose on the thorns and eat the petals as well.

In the back of our house are woods where the deer and the raccoons roam, content to redesign our landscape and redistribute our garbage, but our most troublesome pest, with the possible exception of Pip, proved to be the moth. At first we had no idea what

Taking time to smell the flowers.

Pip was doing, jumping in the air and hopping around in the kitchen, biting at something in the air. He caught on sooner than we did how destructive moths could be. When we finally realized what they were doing to our sweaters, we put a bounty on them.

That night Pip bagged four.

"Score one for the cat," we said. Pip just licked his paw. We were learning to appreciate the little things he did for us.

Pip was approximately two when he came to us. We arbitrarily declared his birthday on the day we first saw him. We bought toys that promised to give Pip "hours of pleasure." He hated them, especially the windup mouse that wouldn't move on carpet. We rolled up balls of yarn, and tossed them for him to chase. He was amused, then annoyed. We were wasting his time. He only became interested in the yarn when I put it away after reading that the fibers could choke a cat. Occasionally, he took a swipe at a toy, though I think he was aiming for us.

Eventually we moved on to catnip. None of that cheap stuff that was diluted with grass clippings. He was definitely interested. He sat on his haunches and looked at the small burlap sack filled with catnip. All at once a white flash flew by me, paws in the air, and took the bag from me. He then proceeded to act very undignified on his back, bag in his mouth, paws clawing at the contents.

Determined that I would have the upper hand, I bought a catnip plant. When I wanted something from him, I planned to pull out the catnip, and he would be putty in my hands. In one sitting Pip devoured the plant, and I lost my best bargaining chip.

Very early on, Pip took walking tours through the house, looking somewhat critically at his new accommodations and my style of housecleaning. We had moved his bed inside the house, but he was on the prowl for better sleeping arrangements, something with a Simmons or Sealy label.

Now that he was landlord and we were tenants, Pip showed us what he thought of his bed by ripping it apart. We admitted that it was probably not suitable for a cat of his sensibilities. He turned his back on me. I knew he was thinking that if I had tried, I could have found him a better bed. After all we were only an hour from Philadelphia, two from New York, and five hours by plane from Los Angeles.

He sat in the living room, staring at the pumpkin rust color of the walls through half-closed, critical eyes. I was beginning to think he wanted us to repaint, until he arched his back and jumped up on a wing chair, turned around in a circle, and curled up. Then he looked up at me and stared at my cluttered desk. Pip proceeded to educate me about the perils of slovenliness. At any other time he could leap between crystal glasses and not break anything, but as he jumped on my desk, he sent pens and papers scattering. Then he stretched out and groomed, knocking my plaque—"A cluttered desk is a sign of genius"—which I had previously misplaced, to the floor. After this workout, he needed a rest, and he headed toward our bedroom.

He wasn't certain about our bed, a four-poster with a canopy and drapes. He climbed on the dresser to get a better view. He contemplated the bed and drapes as only a cat can, giving the impression that he was falling asleep but still taking it all in. It was clear he was worried about the canopy. He didn't like to jump on things that had a lid on top, but the drapes had swinging potential.

He liked the guest room better, and decided that it would be his, except for his evening naps, when he slept with us. He was a ten-pounder who could paralyze us in the night. He slept close to me, his face nestled under my chin, his body on my arm. He would purr loudly, providing the music, while we provided the choreography by stroking him until he fell asleep. In the middle of the night, instead of changing positions, he changed people. He would curl up between my husband's legs. Bob always said that Pip, who appeared to double in weight during the night, knew something about the principles of leverage that he didn't know. In the morning a greatly reduced Pip jumped down onto the bedroom rug.

Pip had a real problem with our choice of rugs. We decided that we did not want wall-to-wall carpet because the floors in our house are random-width pine boards, which had recently been hand sanded. Pip was definitely a carpet cat, the deeper the pile the better. We tried out scatter rugs, new Orientals, and a braided rug that looked as if it had been carried in the back of a pioneer wagon gathering dust along the Cimarron Trail. Pip tested the rugs by sinking his claws into them.

"How about an *old* Oriental?" my husband said. "Maybe he won't be interested in them."

"Charlie Chan? Fu Manchu?"

Pip yawned while Bob ignored me and looked up another rug store in the Yellow Pages.

The next shop was in New Hope. It was filled with

odds and ends of people's lives. "We Buy Everything," a sign said. This was not misleading advertising. We trekked single file through a passageway into a room of carpets hanging on wooden poles. "Stay close," Bob said. "I don't want to lose you."

"This one looks okay," I said. It was threadbare, fringeless, and difficult for Pip to scratch.

"We have better ones," the owner said. "Tabriz. Good quality. Nice animals."

We knew the only animals Pip would appreciate would be mice and birds. "No," we said. "We like this one, or maybe this." Bob pointed to a ripped nine-by-twelve.

"Well, if you two like it," the man said as he rolled up the first rug. He said he wouldn't sell us the damaged carpet. It had been in a barn. "Crazy lady liked horses. Imagine buying a rug for a horse." We didn't tell him about Mr. Picky.

Pip greeted us at the door. As Bob hefted the rug onto his shoulder, I walked ahead, making certain he wouldn't bump into things. Pip watched. It was a division of labor, each according to his own ability.

Bob unrolled the rug. Pip looked as if he expected to find something interesting inside. I smelled mothballs, which were supposed to be offputting to cats. Pip sniffed harder. He was not deterred. That was another theory gone awry. As in the rules of punctuation, to each cat there is an exception.

Pip played with what little fringe there was, as Bob

and I moved around the room, seeing how the color changed. Pip got low to the ground.

"Looks good," Bob said. "Call him and tell him we'll take it."

While I was on the phone, Pip stretched out one claw, then another. He looked defeated. The carpet was tightly woven, with small worn patches. Eventually Pip gave up trying to scratch the carpet. Distressed over his waning influence on us, our basic training was ended. We were now ready for outdoor maneuvers.

We were certain that Pip had led a sheltered life before being tossed out on his own, and that part of the reason he was so thin was that he was not a hunter. He would sit on the terrace grooming, watching the birds and squirrels. He seemed content to let nature walk by undisturbed.

I remember a cat-owning friend of mine telling me that the one thing she never got used to was the sound of the crunching of little mice heads. She thought all cats should come with that warning label.

Previously, I had thought that she was a cultured woman. I thought that was disgusting. "Not Pip," I said. I knew he couldn't prefer mouse when he had Fancy Feast. Only starving cats ate rodents.

She knew better, but had the good sense not to tell me. The best experiences are learned, not anticipated.

The first mouse Pip caught was in our garden, the scene of many of his heroic battles.

It was late fall, and we were raking the leaves, getting

the garden ready for winter. Pip was mesmerized by one pile of leaves. If Monet could have his haystacks, Pip could have his leaf piles. He sniffed and pawed at the leaves, then circled them.

"Maybe there's something in there," I said.

Bob shook his head. He had been raking, and nothing had jumped out, he said.

"Would you, with a cat sitting there?"

We continued to rake. Pip continued to stare. He lay on the ground and pushed his paw into the bottom of the pile, in and out, punching holes in the already brown crumbling leaves.

We scooped the leaves into the cart. We knew that the last pile would probably come with Pip attached.

We began to think he was hallucinating, seeing a mirage of mice. Bob pushed the pile with his rake and before he could say, "See, you silly cat," a mouse ran out toward the vegetable bed with Pip after him.

"I should at least get an assist," Bob said.

When I turned around, Pip had the mouse in his mouth, carrying it the way a mother cat carries kittens.

"At least it was quick," I said as Pip let go of the mouse.

It was then I began to see the maxim "Cat and Mouse" put to work. The mouse was alive. Pip was merciless. He poked at the mouse, batted it with one paw while the animal reared up and squeaked.

Finally the mouse was dead. Pip brought it over to us and dropped it on my foot. "He's bringing you a present," Bob said.

"Next time give him your Bloomies card."

Cats bring offerings in the pagan sense, but they are enlightened enough to know that you will not take them. Pip rubbed up against us, looking for praise. I could see blood on his fur.

Life and death in the country . . . it happens close up with a cat. Pip knew enough to introduce us to blood sports slowly.

The next day Pip left a dead mouse on the doorstep, its little feet up in the air. He began a series of acrobatics, tossing the mouse in the air, batting it with his paws, jumping and catching it. As I went outside to tell him to stop, the mouse whizzed by my head and landed in a yew. Pip retrieved it and continued his athletics. I kept reminding myself that the mouse was already dead.

Pip played the game well, then all of a sudden it was finished. He crouched low on the flagstone path and began to snack. My friend was right about little mouse heads.

I began to worry about Pip eating rodents. They carried disease. I was certain of that, although I wasn't sure what disease. I took his mice away from him, while he made his toilette in preparation for dinner.

I began to look out the window early in the morning to scan the front steps for bodies. When Bob went out the door, I would ask him if he'd mind picking up the dead mouse in much the same way as I would ask him to pick up a quart of milk.

In truth, Pip *liked* to eat mice.

"Mice are nutritious," Dr. Tindall told me. "If the

cat food companies could find a way to package the nutrients in mice, they'd have a great cat food."

I thought of cod, sole, and mouse. Well, maybe.

I let Pip eat a mouse once a week, but not in my presence. Too much of a good thing. Moderation! I was about to tell him of the excesses and the decline of the Roman Empire, but he seemed to be telling me in his way that we should live for the moment.

One spring day when it was turning warm, Pip lined up six mice on the terrace. I was almost getting used to stepping over carcasses to go inside.

I petted Pip and told him he was a wonderful cat. He meowed in agreement.

Being educated by a cat was like learning a foreign language. When you no longer had to translate, when the words came naturally, then you knew you were on the way to real knowledge. It was a significant moment for me, though it mattered little to Pip. He was still basking in his own glory of six in one day.

CHAPTER 4

CALL FORWARDING

*R*oy lives on the top floor of our carriage house. He came with the property, so to speak. A carpenter by trade and an artist by inclination, he had looked after the main house and grounds for the previous owners. After we bought the house, we asked him to stay.

The first time we met Roy we had come back with the real estate agent to look at the house for a second time. "This is Roy," he said without any explanation.

Tall, with a slight hint of a blondish beard, Roy was dressed in a red plaid jacket and baggy khaki trousers with boots just below the knee. His hair was wet and shiny with snow. He had just dismantled an illegal deer blind on the property. One instinctively knows certain things about people. Roy was a kind, good-natured man who happened to love animals. He was also a bachelor with a musical voice.

Once when he was sick—a mere cold, he assured us, sniffling—three women brought him soup. They appeared one after the other at the door to the carriage house. First I saw a blonde go in with a jar of what appeared to be chicken soup, and when I looked again there was a brunette standing at the door with an equally large mason jar. After a third woman appeared, thinner and with a ponytail, I knew the word had been sent out that Roy was sick and home remedies were in order.

Roy appealed to women. At the very least they wanted to mother him, and at the very most to change his bachelor status. The one thing they couldn't do was phone him. Roy did not believe in reaching out and touching someone via plastic and wire.

Bob said he understood, somewhat enviously I think, why Roy did not want a phone. If the amount of traffic on his doorstep was any indication, he would never be off the phone.

Since Bob still worked in New York, we kept our apartment there. Roy looked after the house when we were away, and once Pip acquired us, Roy looked after him. It never occurred to us to bring Pip into the city. He was a country cat. If we had moved out of New York to avoid the hassle, how could we ask him to put up with urban living?

It became evident that Roy needed a phone. After all, when we were away we had to have a method to keep in touch with him to check about the house. I wasn't fooling anyone. The main reason I wanted to call was to find out how Pip was. Despite his solitary months on the road, Pip needed me, and I needed him.

We were worried that if we had two listings under our name, especially one that said carriage house, it might conjure up illusions of grandeur to those who scanned phonebooks for profit. We decided to get Roy an unlisted number. After the phone company told us the high cost of anonymity, we tried to find another way to keep Roy's name out of the fine print of the directory. It seemed silly to pay hush money.

Bob looked upon the project as a challenge, and he made a list that began with Arnold, B and ended with Zapata, V. My list was more mundane, but we were convinced that with a minimum amount of trouble and expense, we would have a phone and Roy could keep his privacy.

One night while we were discussing the merits of acronyms versus literary names, Pip rubbed up against us. He was taking his nightly constitutional across our desk. He stopped to scratch his ear before attacking the phone cord as if it were a snake. When he saw it was neither alive nor interesting, he scratched his head on the receiver.

There was our answer. The suave, debonair P. Le Chat, cat about town, would be Roy's *nom de phone*. It seemed simple at the time, trouble-free. Bob was delighted that his three years of French were not wasted.

We informed Pip that he would soon have what every teenager wanted—his own phone. We warned him about dialing those 900 numbers and listening to the purring. He took it in stride and washed his face the whole time we talked to him.

I called the phone company the next day. Mr. Le

Chat could be dialing within a couple of days. All the company needed was a copy of the last three months of phone bills from Mr. Le Chat's previous address.

"I'm sorry, that's not possible," I said, stumbling over my words. "He only used pay phones before. What I mean is, in his line of work he . . ." I was making it worse. At first he sounded like a reclusive superman, and now I was giving him an occupation that at best sounded indictable. "I'll vouch for Mr. Le Chat," I said. "The bills will be coming to me."

"I see."

She probably thought she had discovered P. Le Chat's line of work — blackmail.

"Is that one name? First initial P as in . . ."

"Pierre?" I said.

"Do you want Pierre spelled out?"

"No, he prefers only an initial."

I had to spell the name twice. The first time I misspelled it by adding an extra vowel. Bob kept pantomiming, pointing to his eye, and saying no.

She repeated the spelling back to me. "C-H-A-T, no 'I.' Lay Chat. He's a foreigner, isn't he?"

Since the breakup of the phone company everything is extra. Did he want a maintenance contract, a touch tone? We realized that it would be easier for him to use, but we decided on a basic rotary phone. No, he did not have a computer or fax, and he probably wouldn't be making more than a hundred dollars worth of business calls to one area code. At least we hoped he wouldn't.

Mr. Le Chat's credit was impeccable, and an installer could be there the following day. With a name like that the phone company probably thought he would be immediately dialing France.

Shortly before noon, the start of Pip's afternoon siesta, Bell of Pennsylvania pulled into the driveway. Pip, who had a low opinion of all motor vehicles, sprawled in my flower bed on top of Mrs. R. H. Gray, crushing the pink blossoms of the prize-winning heather. When I came out, Pip made his move like a commando. As the man put down his toolbox, Pip jumped on top, spread-eagle.

"Nice cat," the man said. "Mr. Le Chat?" I was surprised by his insight, but he was not looking at Pip. "Mr. Le Chat?" he said again.

"No, he's out." By now Pip was sitting at the foot of the carriage-house stairs, eyes half open. Obviously, we were keeping him awake with this unnecessary talk.

"We have a service order. Installation. Mr. Le Chat called and said someone could let us in if he wasn't here."

I nodded.

Pip was becoming bored. He purred and rubbed up against the man's leg. He was clearly out to annoy Baby Bell.

"Nice cat," the man said. "Is he allowed in?"

"Yes, of course," I said. "Mr. Le Chat likes cats."

The man nodded as Pip ran up the stairs and into

Roy's apartment. "Makes himself right at home, doesn't he?"

As he was putting in the jack, he patted Pip and gently nudged him off Roy's chair. "Nice cat," he said again. Pip jumped up on the desk and sat on the man's toolbox again. "Are you sure he's allowed in here?"

I nodded and removed Mr. Le Chat from the desk. He had a plastic bag with a modular jack caught on his claws. I handed the man the bag.

"He's a reader," the man said, looking at Roy's bookcase. "All these books. Twain. *The Three Musketeers.*"

I thought of all the books that I had been trying to read that Pip sat on. Yes, he clearly was a reader.

"You can tell a lot about a person by what he reads. Some places I go, no books. But Mr. Le Chat, now he's a reader." When he started to ask where to send the bill, Pip scooted out the door.

Since Roy's line also rang in our house, we answered his calls during the day when he was out.

Roy didn't have to worry about people bothering him. Most of the calls were for Pip. It never occurred to us that anyone would want to talk to a cat.

"Is Mr. Le Chat there?"

"I'm sorry. He can't come to the phone now." I couldn't tell the man that he was out chasing mice. Gardening sounded better. "He's outside gardening," I finally said.

"When do you expect him in?"

I offered to take a message and assured him that

Pip was an avid reader.

Mr. Le Chat was very busy, and no, he did not have a car phone. "How could he?" I wanted to say. "He's afraid to ride in cars."

The man was a stockbroker and insisted that Pip should have a professional manage his portfolio. After all, the market was tough and he could put Mr. Le Chat into low-risk, high-yield investments.

I told him that I was certain Mr. Le Chat took care of his own investments. When he called back later that afternoon, Bob told him that Pip was bearish about the market, and was keeping all his assets in cash.

The next day the broker was euphoric. There was a new issue coming out at twenty dollars a share, and only a few select clients were being advised. He expected the stock to be worth twenty-five within a few months. Pip could take a capital gain and put the funds in a money market account.

"Now I'm going out on a limb telling him this," he said.

By now Pip was also out on a limb. A squirrel had disturbed his nap, and he retaliated by chasing it up a tree.

"Mr. Le Chat could make a killing," he said.

Pip had already made several big killings, I said, but I refused to elaborate.

"Since you are an associate . . ." Yesterday he assumed I was Pip's secretary, but since I had evidently been promoted he did not mind discussing "good as gold" high-yield bonds to finance takeovers, a "steal," he said. Precisely the words I would have used.

He reminded me of Pip, sitting on the edge of a field, waiting patiently for his next victim to come along.

"Does Mr. Le Chat have a first name?" he asked.

"Yes," I said, and let it go.

Roy began to get phone calls at night.

"Mr. Le Chat, I'm glad to finally get to talk to you. Your secretary [I'd been demoted] said English wasn't your native language, so I'm going to take things slow.

Now I understand you're illiquid at this point. I suggest reducing your equities, and holding thirty percent cash for the right deal."

A few days later a package arrived for Pip. It was an oil and gas investment—a working interest in a well to be drilled in Oklahoma. Only twenty thousand a unit. Pip was definitely a high roller. Naturally we showed him the prospectus. Tampering with the mail was a federal offense. He was nonplussed. The only thing that interested him in the ground was a mole.

The man followed up the prospectus with a phone call.

Being raised in a small town, I was not taught the fine art of saying no. When I first moved to New York, I talked to mumblers and answered the rhetorical questions of people who were looking for God. I was certainly no match for Pip's callers.

Even the postal service was interested in Pip. Our mail box was filling up with junk mail, most of it for P. Le Chat and any other name variation from Pee Shot to Pao De Chat to Pablo Cat. Among the letters, which seemed to be addressed to the various members of the U.N. delegation, was an application for an insurance policy. There were the basic questions— height, weight. On a separate page were questions intended for "informational purposes only." How often did Pip eat red meat? How much alcohol did he consume per day, per week? Did he use drugs? Did he smoke? We thought of filling out the application.

His weight alone would probably alarm the actuaries, unless of course they took his height into consideration.

Within a few months Pip was on everyone's mailing list. He was offered charge acounts and told that he was a valued customer. His preapproved credit line on VISA was larger than mine initially was. He was entered in a sweepstakes and warned that if he, P. Le Chat, did not send his coupon in the very next day he would be losing out on a million dollars. It was not necessary to buy a subscription to a magazine, the letter indicated, but it seemed to increase his chances.

Our mailbox was jammed with duplicate catalogues. Most were still addressed to us, but since Pip was a new customer, as one company put it, and "we want to get your business," he was entitled to a free gift of half a pound of corn-cured bacon. It didn't seem quite fair because we knew who would be paying the bills. Then the moment we waited for came. Mrs. P. Le Chat started using our address as a mail drop.

If nothing else, the insurance salesman was persistent. He warned Mrs. Le Chat about the horrors of her husband losing his job, or worse yet having an accident. How would they pay hospitalization, the mortgage? We assured Pip that we would never kick him out. Mrs. Le Chat, whoever she was, was a different matter.

Mrs. Le Chat had apparently been busy. Charge accounts were waiting for her at Sears, Texaco, and

Wanamaker's. In addition she had won a television set—no strings attached, only wires we hoped. All she had to do was drive to the Poconos to a real estate development and show her letter with Urgent stamped across it in blood red to Mr. X. While she was there, it was strongly suggested that she take the personal prearranged tour of the luxurious houses on half an acre. "We are sure you will agree that the homesites are of incomparable beauty. Be sure and bring two ID's, so your special prize will be given only to you."

Bus schedules from Doylestown were included in case she did not want to drive. Mrs. Le Chat would be met in an air-conditioned van, and if she could not personally pick up her twelve-inch portable, her husband could. We thought about Pip getting his own television, but we were already too indulgent.

Neither Le Chat made the trip to the Poconos, and we were lucky that we didn't have to guarantee a mortgage on a half-acre lot in the Poconos. Pip had expensive tastes and would probably have chosen the model with the giant Jacuzzi in the master bathroom.

A few days later, Mrs. Le Chat received a threatening mailgram on yellow paper, probably a not-so-subtle hint about the quality of the language contained inside. This was definitely the last notice for one Mrs. Pee Lechat.

By now "*You* could have won not only the television, but a Jeep Cherokee and $7,500." The jeep was tan and silver.

If she acted now and called the operator standing by, she would receive His and Her matching sports watches.

Pip wasn't interested. Time was immaterial to him, and he hadn't seen hide nor hair of the Mrs. for days.

CHAPTER 5

RUNNING AN INFIRMARY

*I*t was naive of us to think that Pip had survived his walk on the wild side due only to the kindness of strangers. He was a hunter, and after he regained his strength everything on our property was fair game.

Although I did not expect Pip to look upon wildlife with the same awe as I did, I did expect him to show some restraint. I was troubled by his scorched-earth policy. It was a dilemma. Cats, when left to their own devices, kill other animals. While I tried to preach the pacifist doctrine, Bob promoted Darwin, the survival of the fittest, the law of natural selection. I was determined not to interfere with nature, but I did have trouble with the idea that Pip was the selector and that most of his selections appeared on our doorstep.

Most of the time I remained nonaligned, although I protected Mr. and Mrs. Cardinal who regularly dined alfresco beneath our bird feeders. Mrs. Cardinal was not only a less flashy dresser than her mate, she was also slow.

*We moved the feeder higher once we realized it
attracted a big white bird.*

Pip routinely ambushed her. He hid under the
porch benches, white body crouched, black tail moving. I sabotaged his efforts. Banged doors. Sang old
camp songs. Appealed to the romantic in him. "They
mate for life," I said. I should have realized that
romantic notion had limited appeal to a neutered cat.

As I was doing the dishes one morning, I heard a
screech. Someone was rehearsing the murder scene in

Macbeth in our yard. I was certain that Pip was playing a major role, so I hurried outside.

Pip was arching his back and diving into the boxwoods. By the way he batted his paws I knew that there was something in the bushes.

"Now, Pip," I said, about to begin my abbreviated lecture on the sanctity of animal life. I was certain the cardinals were not in jeopardy, so I excluded the birds and the bees. "Come here."

He looked at me, than took a swing at the box-wood. Another shriek.

I walked around the bush three times before I saw a small pair of eyes looking back at me.

Pip seemed irritated. He glared at me and turned his head toward the garden.

Last night something had pilfered our lettuce. Though we did not lift any pawprints, the heist had all the earmarks of a bunny. That morning Bob and I had talked about ways to protect our garden from rabbits, and now I had the answer brushing up against me, purring. Pip was prepared to help us in any way he could. From his point of view the condemned had already eaten a hearty meal. I picked up the quivering bunny, while Pip followed behind.

When I was growing up, a farmer cut our fields and used the hay to feed his cattle. Unfortunately, his tractor sometimes disturbed a rabbit's nest, and the mother never returned, leaving her babies to starve.

My mother took in the orphans. I remember

watching her feed the bunnies, their eyes closed, with a dropper of milk laced with whisky. She had learned that odd concoction not from her teetotaler father, but from a neighbor whose child was born prematurely. Take her home, the hospital said, meaning of course to let her die. From the day the baby came home her mother fed her milk and good Irish whisky. The baby eventually played on our high school's basketball team. Mother had no such aspirations for the bunnies. She turned them loose when they were old enough to take care of themselves, and before, as my father put it, mixing animal metaphors, they could get into any monkey business.

Bob experienced bunnies suburban style. He was brought up in the wilds of West Hartford where rabbits came in cages and were rumored to do stuff at night behind bars, a morality lesson that was not wasted on young teenage boys. The bunnies were in cages for a reason.

Pip no doubt had his own ideas about bunnies.

I took the bunny upstairs to a bathroom, put a towel down on the floor, and turned on the lights to give it warmth. Then I set out to find its nest with the help of Pip.

He was only too happy to act as my guide, and offered various solutions to the problem of alternative housing. We walked through the fields. I looked underneath the apple trees but rejected that site as being too open, offering no protection from predators. The red-tailed hawk's nest in the nearby spruce hardly augured well for the friendliness of the neighbors. Having just bought a house, perhaps I was a little too particular. I was looking not only for a view, but other amenities as well. Besides, I had forgotten what a rabbit's warren looked like. I finally gave up. Pip seemed to take my failings in his stride, and he walked along behind me, sniffing, giving every aborted home site the once-over.

I tried to find my copy of *Watership Down*, and when I couldn't, I asked Bob if he remembered anything about the book.

He shook his head and then asked if it was about a sunken U-Boat. "I'm going to call Dr. Tindall," I said.

"Do you think he's read it?"

I ignored him and dialed. I was beginning to worry that he would have an unlisted number by now.

"I have this bunny," I said. I didn't need to go into explanations.

"How big is the rabbit?" he said.

"I don't know. Smaller than a bread box. Fits in my palm."

It seemed from the description that the bunny was about three weeks old. It could hop, open its eyes, take food, and scratch.

I had two choices—three, if I considered Pip's. I could take care of the bunny until it was large enough to escape from predators, or you know who. That would be about two to three months, or I could let it go in a cozy habitat when Pip was asleep. It probably would survive on its own until it found its mother.

Somehow I couldn't see raising a rabbit in a guest bathroom. I had visions of saying to friends who were coming to visit us that weekend: "Here's your bathroom. Towels are here, soap, bunny, bathmat."

I sat down and considered the options. The bunny had stopped shaking. Obviously, it didn't see the white paws poking underneath the door. When I do not know what to do with an animal, I feed it. I suppose it's wishful thinking that if I were ever lost someone would do the same for me. I put milk on my finger and the bunny licked.

I waited for Pip to take his leisurely afternoon nap. Eventually, he fell asleep on our bed. I knew if I kept the bunny any longer, I'd have to get it a Social Security number, so I took it down the back staircase and out to the woods, using enough maneuvers so Pip could not trace its scent. I was getting dizzy. If I kept zigzagging, I knew I'd need a compass to find my way back. I put the rabbit in the field underneath a bush. I kept telling him what a wonderful new home he had and that he should go west, east, any direction except toward the boxwood to seek his fortune. The bunny hopped into the underbrush. He was going to live.

I went out to the garden in the late afternoon while Pip was still sleeping. In the boxwood was the bunny curled up in the same place.

"Get lost. Go away," I yelled. The ingrate

scratched me as I pulled it from the boxwood. I took the rabbit back to his new home and told him firmly to stay there. It looked at me with beady eyes. I was not about to argue with a dumb bunny — none of this pussyfooting around. This was serious business — life and death. "Don't move," I said. I put a fence around the boxwood. If the bunny was going to meet its end, it would not be in our tree.

I kept Pip in all night. Even a tunafish bribe was eaten begrudgingly. By the way he stared at me between bites, I knew I had failed him again.

Months later when I was outside I saw two bunnies hopping by the boxwood. They stopped and looked, and for a moment I thought it was our bunny — Pip's and mine — showing his friend the family tree.

In the early summer, as I was still basking in my animal rescue mission, Pip found some baby birds that had fallen out of their nest. He delivered the birds to us on the back terrace one after another. One was dead.

We followed him to see where his supply of birds was coming from and saw that the nest was high up in a cherry tree. Apparently, the birds were on the verge of learning to fly and had fallen out of the nest.

We thought of getting a ladder and putting the remaining bird back in the nest. I was an expert tree climber in my youth, and even though I was taller now, so were the trees. I was not about to relive my lost tree-climbing days on a seventy-foot sycamore.

*Pip looking for feathered friends to bring to
the infirmary.*

Our longest extension ladder could reach only halfway up, and there was only one Huxley agile enough to jump to the higher branches.

Pip was a sucker for ladders. Once when men were fixing the roof of our barn, Pip climbed their ladder and went to sleep on the rafters. Luckily, they saw him before they nailed on the cedar shingles.

Bob got the ladder anyway and put it against the tree, looked up, and said, "Maybe." Then he looked again and said, "Maybe not." Pip was already on the third rung, when Bob grabbed him.

While Bob went upstairs with Pip to get the sickroom ready, I called the good doctor. He was less optimistic about my rearing a baby bird. The bird probably was injured from the fall, even though I saw no marks. It needed to be fed every three hours, water and mashed up worms, or minute amounts of cat food.

I took a basket and filled it with grass clippings and straw, then lifted the bird in. It was so tiny. Its feathers stuck up like a bad crewcut.

I put a tensor lamp nearby for warmth and opened a can of cat food. I took out tiny amounts of food, tapped on the beak the way the mother bird does, and put food in when it opened its mouth. It squeaked again and I fed it.

I remembered Bob's mother telling me how finicky he was about eating his vegetables. She was certain that he would come down with one of those nineteenth century diseases such as scurvy or rickets. At mealtime she played "Go fishing" with Bob. With a fork as a fishing pole and vegetable as bait, she was out to hook Bob on greenery.

"Be firm, but gentle," Bob said, "but most of all sincere." It was tough to be sincere in a bathroom with a bird.

I held the bird in my hand. It fluttered and opened its mouth. As I tapped on its beak again, I began to think how similar child-rearing methods are. "I'm going fishing," I said, and the bird opened its mouth.

I looked around. In the sink was my furry white assistant, quietly crouching, trying to blend in with the porcelain. He meowed his best meow, but I wasn't so easily fooled. He was up to no good. I put him outside and shut the door. Usually, he would have huffed off to sulk at such an affront, but he stayed outside, meowing sweetly.

I looked around at the bathroom. If we kept this up, Bob and I would have to consider setting up our own HMO, and offering group rates.

The bird squeaked, tottered across the wooden floor, trying to keep its balance, and curled up on the towel.

I fed it during the night and made certain that the tensor lamp was not too close.

In the morning, Pip was outside the bathroom door, standing guard. He expected to be rewarded in some, yet undetermined, way.

I found the bird, cold, curled up on a towel, its mouth open as if it were waiting to be fed. I buried the bird away from its nest, near a stream, with a clear view of the open sky.

Fifty percent, I thought. I tried to be content with those odds until Pip found his next victim.

The squirrels had it in for Pip, although I suppose he was not entirely blameless. They tormented him, bombarding him with nuts and bark. They dumped pine cones on his head, and made rude noises whenever he came near. They seemed to be able to calculate how close they could get to a sleeping cat without waking him and suffering his revenge.

After a storm when the gutters overflowed, the squirrels cleaned them out by raining pine needles down on Pip's head.

He took all these indignities in his stride by trying to find ways to kill them. He hid in yews, waiting to bushwhack them on their favorite trails.

We had a guerilla war in our yard. All weapons of war were allowed. There was no civility left among the combatants.

The gray squirrels patrolled the backyard. More laid back than their red counterparts, less schooled in the art of cat baiting, they made mistakes.

A cat follows movement, and one particularly inept squirrel would crawl down the trunk of a large ash and remain perfectly still except for its swishing tail. Pip would sit at the bottom and jump up.

I watched this game every day, often refereeing when things got too rough. All right, I felt like saying, illegal tail grabbing.

One day the squirrel, a bit too cocky from his earlier triumphs, climbed farther down the trunk. Pip grabbed its tail and hung on. As the squirrel scurried back up, Pip removed most of the hair from its tail.

A few days later a decorator came to the house to show me fabric samples for curtains. I had hoped that I would be able to make curtains for our house, a nice homey touch, but Bob knew my way with a needle and said that he did not want sheets stapled to the windows. In college, I Scotchtaped hems and glued on buttons. Besides, our house was pre-Revolutionary, and I wasn't certain what type of curtains, if any, would look appropriate.

"Swags and jabots," the decorator had suggested over the phone. Somehow that sounded like the posturing that was going on in our yard between Pip and the squirrels.

As the decorator got out of the car, I saw Pip lunge for something.

A baby squirrel fell from a high branch and into the waiting paws. Squirrels from heaven, Pip must have thought. He batted the baby squirrel and cut its back leg.

"Excuse me," I said. She stood there, holding a book of material samples while I did laps around the house after Pip.

I returned with a wiggling, frightened squirrel in my hand, cat at my feet, hissing. I smiled at her. "Be right back. I have to take the squirrel to the bathroom."

I left Pip to explain. When I returned, he was sitting under the tree waiting for good fortune to hit him on the head again.

"Now about the curtains?" she said. I think she was afraid to ask me any other questions.

While we were talking, the squirrel shredded a roll of toilet paper and clawed a bar of Royal Gardenia soap. I was glad to see that it was well enough to be treated on an outpatient basis.

The decorator never asked me what I was doing with a squirrel in our bathroom. By now Pip was turning us into converts. We had tried unsuccessfully to curb his aggressive instincts. When mole season rolled around again, we decided to enlist his help.

The moles had appropriated our yard. Their tunnels crisscrossed our lawn, leaving unhealthy dirt on top, we were told. Our lawn was actually a sort of meadow with clover, crabgrass, and weeds, and every now and then a respectable blade of real grass.

Each day we stomped down the mounds. If nothing else we would deafen the little buggers. I had some sympathy. They were already blind.

Our desperation was in direct proportion to the number of new tunnels. If they weren't digging to China, they were definitely going somewhere.

Our neighbors suggested putting smoke bombs in the holes. Our industrious moles probably already had escape routes in the event of a fire.

"What do you do when they escape?" we asked.

"Shoot them."

Great! A massacre in our yard.

"Or poison them," our neighbors said. "But the best deterrent . . ."

We could hardly wait. Chemical warfare was probably next. We were surprised when they said, "A cat."

Our expectations built over the winter. We had our deterrent resting up. Pip was a natural. If he wanted to kill and maim, who were we to stop him? We would just be more specific about his targets. We waited for mole day with anticipation.

Eventually, Pip got his first mole. He brought it to us, squirming. I was not about to rush in with a gurney. I felt somewhat barbaric rooting for him to kill another animal, but I looked at my flower bed. Of the two hundred bulbs I had planted, there weren't many survivors. I knew this mole could not be entirely responsible, but he was at least a willing accomplice. Pip dropped the mole at our feet. In the hierarchy of cuteness, moles are definitely at the bottom, but creatures should not be done away with because they are ugly. Otherwise, many of us wouldn't be here.

Pip poked at the mole, who played dead. He picked it up in his mouth again and put it down—a new location to initiate the chase. Nothing. The slug just lay there. Again Pip changed his venue. Again nothing. By now Bob and I felt like Romans in the stands encouraging gladiators. "Thumbs down," we yelled. Pip ignored us, and then, to our amazement, he ignored the mole. They were obviously too dull for him.

Not only did Pip leave the mole alive and healthy, he left it near a mound of dirt. The mole didn't even have to take the underground to his tunnels. They were right there.

Though we were disappointed not to have a solution to the mole problem, we were pleased that our pacifist instructions had taken hold. Pip looked at us as only a cat could do, with contempt bordering on eventual forgiveness. While we were still shaking our heads, feeling the earth move under our feet—something that used to hold a different meaning for us—Pip took off after a squirrel.

The infirmary was open again.

CHAPTER 6

MOBILE VET

*A*fter we moved from New York to the peace and comfort of country living, and before Pip came to live with us and protect the premises, we decided we needed an alarm system. Confronted with a long drive-way and a forest behind and beside us, we began to wonder about the wisdom of exchanging the cloistered environment of an apartment for life in the woods.

Reading the town newspaper only confirmed what we had feared—New Hope was in the midst of a crime wave. The previous weekend "person(s) unknown had removed three zinnias from a porch," and "person(s) unknown had thrown half a pink grapefruit at a woman." We knew it was only a matter of time before the perpetrator(s) turned from botany to larceny.

I called several alarm companies. One touted dogs from West Germany that would live with you. Whether we wanted them to or not, we thought. Another recommended four-inch decals on every win-dow warning an intruder not to enter—probably the same success rate as a cross to ward off Dracula.

I eventually talked to the nearest company, which advertised sturdy locks and an unobtrusive tear gas system, and made an appointment.

As we walked into the office, the owner asked us if we liked animals. I was afraid I had called the wrong company, so I nodded vigorously. There was a playpen near his desk. I looked inside, and the baby barked at me.

Other dogs began appearing, nursemaids, it seemed, to the latest addition—a puppy that had been thrown from a car into traffic. "They're real overprotective," the owner said, as I backed away from the boxer. "Now let me show you something."

We thought we were about to get down to the nuts and dead bolts of the security business. Instead, he wrote a name and phone number on a piece of paper and said that since we liked animals, sooner or later one would come our way, and that if we needed a veterinarian, Dr. Tindall was the best.

"He makes housecalls."

At the time we wondered what kind of a person would make housecalls other than a plumber or an electrician.

I filed Dr. Tindall's number in a stack of papers and forgot about it until Pip straggled onto our porch. He was so emaciated and sickly that I couldn't imagine taking him to a doctor's office. Every time I touched Pip, fur came off in my hands.

I retrieved Dr. Tindall's number from my files and

called. All we wanted at the time was for him to tell us that Pip was going to live and that he did not have some infectious disease. Tindall told us later that he thought that Pip, the purported barn cat, was already a part of our family. He said he recognized the symptoms: the meal of scrambled eggs, the scientific testing of cat food, and the overprotective look of a new mother.

Over the years and the medical crises, we began to know Dr. Tindall as Ed. I knew I liked him personally as well as professionally, when one day after he had given Pip his yearly vaccinations, Pip rubbed up against him sweetly, then clawed him. Tindall said he was glad to see that Pip had gotten back to his fighting weight and patted him on his head.

What intrigued us most was Dr. Tindall's moveable office. Though he had a clinic adjacent to his home, he preferred to treat animals in their own surroundings and not in an office setting. It seemed a sensible approach, though unusual. After Pip recovered and was no longer docile and maleable (if he ever was), he would have been impossible to take to a veterinarian's office. He hated cars and would have disliked an office filled with other animals even more. Having a doctor come to the house alleviated part of the distress. In addition, when there was more than one animal, all the animals could be vaccinated at once.

Dr. Tindall describes himself as basically a New Jersey boy who grew up in Grover's Mills, the location

Pip rarely posed for formal portraits.

of Orson Welles' radio production of *The War of the Worlds*. "Nothing much happened except for a few Martians landing . . . or so I've heard," he said. He was a baby at the time, and missed the only real excitement in the town.

By the time he applied to veterinary school, he had a masters degree in medical entomology. At that time there were only eighteen veterinary schools in the country, and about two hundred applicants for every position.

"They did everything to discourage you," he said. "It was difficult back then in the dark ages."

His first veterinary job was in practice with a well-respected Princeton veterinarian. "People loved him, and when they came in, they'd stare at me and wonder who I was, and think maybe their animal could wait."

After a year he went into practice on his own in Lambertville, a once-thriving Jersey town on the Delaware River, in a room big enough for one person and a couple of large dogs. He thought at first that there wouldn't be much business, but he was inundated. He would get to work about seven and leave late. He rarely saw his children. "They were young then," he said, "not teenagers. I wanted to see them."

He had a few surprises in his practice. "It was during the hippie era. I couldn't diagnose the bizarre symptoms until I learned how to ask the right questions, such as what kind of brownies did the dog eat last night?"

It was during that time that Tindall began to think about having a veterinary service that came to the patient. People used to call his office at all hours and say that their dog had just gotten sick, or it had just fallen. "I knew it happened earlier and they just got around to noticing." He began to see patterns. "People are on their best behavior in a doctor's office. It's somewhat intimidating, and people are reluctant to admit they left the cap off medicine, or fell asleep with the animal outside."

After six years of a hectic, yet profitable — ("This was the most money I ever made.") — existence, he decided to see if there was a need for a mobile vet. He had a market study done, based on demographics and economics, to see if it was practical. He was worried about supporting a family.

"There were no yardsticks to go by. I doubt if there were more than four practices like this in the entire country back in 1975."

Tindall uses a modified van similar to a commercially produced motor home as a mobile office. He covers a radius of about fifteen miles. There are stainless steel counters in his van, an operating table, and a few cages for the animals he boards. One wall is covered with cartoons, although Garfield is conspicuously absent. Many of the graphics selected by his wife concern a workaholic.

Shortly after he started his practice, he moved to an old stone house with a barn and a lot of land. Before long he became the local SPCA, the doc at the end of a dead-end country road. At one time he had over thirteen barn cats. People would drop off animals.

"I'd look out in the yard and see another cat, sometimes with only one ear or an eye. A bunch of them together would make a whole cat."

People not only brought domestic animals, but wild

and orphaned animals as well. Fawns appeared on his doorstep, dropped off by well-meaning people and even some guilty hunters.

Buttercup was his favorite fawn. As a youngster, she would butt the front door of their house or raise her foot and bang on the window and insist on coming inside. She loved dry cereal and barked until she was given her own bowl. She ate quickly, because the indoor cats annoyed her.

As she grew older she would leave for longer periods of time, until finally she joined a herd. She frequently returned for a visit, and picnickers would find her near Tindall's house. Often from the city, these people developed a rather idealized view of how Bambi survived in the wilds of New Jersey.

Though he took his children with him in the van when they were young, he is used to working alone, which is contrary to the way most veterinarians are taught. Even the prescribed method of administering anesthesia involves two people: one holds the animal, while the other gives the medication. Tindall has always combined the two.

Once when Tindall was on vacation, I called another veterinarian and explained that Pip had a tick at the corner of his eye and that I was afraid to use a tweezer to remove it. I explained that our vet was away, and after expressing surprise about a doctor who made housecalls, the veterinarian said he could fit us in, but Pip, a wild cat he presumed from my description, would have to be anesthetized. Following instructions Tindall had given once before, Bob and I overcame our fear and removed the tick, sparing Pip the additional trauma of an office visit and medication.

When asked if he remembered the first strange reaction he got when he told someone he made house-calls, he laughed and said he still gets that reaction, even from veterinarians. He realizes he is controversial, but he believes he can provide good service for less cost. The other services are always available.

"If I didn't believe in what I was doing, and that I was capable, I wouldn't have the mobile service." He feels it is a matter of perspective. "You have to have confidence in an owner's ability to care for his pet."

There are many procedures he will perform only in his clinic, such as orthopedic surgery. He would not want to discharge animals to their owners immediately without making certain that everything was aligned and that there was no rise in temperature or unusual swelling.

Every animal reacts differently to medication, due to metabolism, body weight, and physiological make-up. There are guidelines, and he tells the owners what to watch for, and to call him immediately if there are any unusual developments. He has a cellular phone in his van, and he tells his clients that he is available anytime. "Why make a sick animal wait because it's a weekend?"

Many of the same issues confront both the medical

practitioner and the veterinarian. Technological advancements have made it easier to detect and treat illnesses and to a lesser extent prolong a greatly diminished quality of life. Many believe that if a doctor or a hospital does not have the latest equipment, they will receive inadequate treatment. It is a dilemma for the practitioner, because once the equipment is acquired, it must be used to justify the expense. Technology also gives owners an expectation that animals can be saved from most illnesses or accidents.

Dr. Tindall and I have had many philosophical discussions in our kitchen, with Pip looking on. Even though he was a relatively young cat, I told Tindall that I had a fear of losing Pip, not in the sense of misplacing him, though in a cluttered house and with a cat's ability to hide it might be possible. I could not bring myself to say, "When Pip died, when he became infirm." What I did tell Tindall was that I wanted to keep Pip with me always, whatever the cost.

"What about Pip?" he said one day. Pip was jumping up in the air, batting an imaginary opponent. "What about the quality of his life?"

I shook my head and let Tindall speak.

Tindall believes in aggressive treatment as long as the quality of life for the animal is improved. Insulin, heart medication, such as the digitalis that was prescribed for Bob's childhood dog, is recommended, even chemotherapy. If the treatment only prolongs the agony and is intended to make the owner feel better, Tindall recommends against it.

If a terminally ill animal cannot be treated at home, he monitors it in his clinic and calls the family when death is imminent so that they can be with the animal at the end. That way he can keep the animal comfortable and out of as much pain as possible and let the family be with it. He knows the importance of being with a dying animal.

At one time the Tindalls owned two Manx cats named Bonnie and Clyde. Clyde, the bigger one, was black with a stumpy tail. They were let out during the day, and they rarely strayed. One afternoon Bonnie returned without her sidekick.

The Tindalls searched that night and the next morning for Clyde, making certain that he was not hit by a car, or hurt. Though illegal, there were still some old leghold traps, hidden by the undergrowth, in the woods. Handwritten signs went up in the grocery stores. As the summer progressed, they continued to look for Clyde.

Meanwhile, neighbors down the road had left on vacation, and a woman was house-sitting for them and their cat who was black with a normal tail. The woman knew little about cats. She was a musician and was preoccupied with classical music. The first day she was there the cat got out.

The next morning, she saw a black tailless cat, jumping on some logs. She tried to entice it inside with food, with a catnip toy. She tried netting it. Finally, she caught her ward, and brought him into the house. The woman was amazed that the cat, who obviously had been in an accident and lost its tail, was able to heal so quickly.

When the owners returned, they were amazed to see their cat reincarnated, but Clyde was such fun that they adopted him.

Eventually, the Tindalls heard this strange story, of the cat that lost its tail, but by then their neighbors were on another vacation. Clyde was alive and summering on the Jersey shore. The Tindalls were determined to get Clyde back. They went down to the shore to confront the cat burglars. They showed them a series of mug shots and brought Clyde back to Bonnie.

Unfortunately, Clyde had developed a urinary infection, not uncommon in male cats, which is treatable if detected early. As much as he tried, Tindall could not save Clyde. He was painfully aware, he said, of the irony of being a veterinarian who could not save his own animal.

CHAPTER 7

CROSSING THE BORDER

*M*y paternal grandfather was an avid fisherman. By profession he was an attorney, but he put as much enthusiasm into catching speckled trout as he did into the practice of law.

In the late twenties, after hearing a fish tale from a reliable source, he drove twenty hours straight over bad roads to a lake, only to be told that in another lake six hours north of Toronto, the fish were bigger. Prizefighters, he remembered the man saying.

The next year he lured Grandmother to the lake. The year after that he built a summer house—a fishing camp, he called it—on Kaminiskeg Lake. In Algonquin Indian, it meant the lake of the wild geese. Grandfather always thought it was a mistranslation, and substituted the word "fish" for geese. Since roads had not reached that part of the lake, the only access then was by boat.

It was a time when big sprawling houses were built. The design was a rectangle, with a central living room and bedrooms on either side. Grandfather swore he had made the blueprint on a paper bag, and the workmen followed his architectural plan. Grandmother penciled in the amenities—indoor plumbing and a separate wing for their five boys.

I have spent part of every summer in that house since I was two. As a child I enjoyed hot weather, bathing suits, and noisy cousins. Now I prefer September, when the tourists have gone and the leaves are in color.

Although we had never traveled anywhere with Pip, I could not imagine leaving him. My father-in-law had recently stayed with us, and Pip, in one of his more perverse moods, had waited until late at night to jump on his bed, walk across his stomach, then jump down. He suggested that if we wanted to take Pip, or that "Awful cat," as he called him, to Canada, we should consider leaving him there. He was convinced that Pip would ruin our vacation. I was equally convinced that I would miss Pip too much.

Even though Pip, as I have said, had definite opinions about cars—he hated all of them—we decided that he should go with us to Canada.

Since the cottage was five hundred miles from home, backpacking was out of the question, especially when we considered what we were taking with us.

Pip's baggage was substantial. Cat litter and litter box, scratching post, a bed cushion—our canopy bed where he usually slept was too large to put in the car—toys, and cases of his food. The vet had warned us that cats' stomachs were delicate and that they did

not like a change in their diet. I never could understand how anything that ate a mouse, fur and all, could
be said to have a delicate stomach.

Pip was uneasy when the suitcases came out of the
closet, probably because he thought something would
fall on him. He was even more upset when I started to
pack, and he retreated underneath a bed.

Being able to revise his plans immediately, he
jumped into the suitcase and peered over the edge,
almost daring me to continue. So far I had packed a
pair of jeans, a sweatshirt, and Pip.

*We often had to let the cat out of the bag to
continue packing.*

I left him alone and went to count out his cans of food. I figured five cans a day to be safe.

"That's ridiculous," Bob said. "*We* couldn't even eat that much a day." Since I was in charge of the cat food, I ignored Bob and put in five cans a day, plus an extra week's supply. I figured if my appetite increased dramatically in Canada, why couldn't Pip's.

We loaded the car during one of Pip's naps, which gave us ample time. Our car is a station wagon with an enormous well that I filled immediately with essentials such as old New Yorkers — Does anyone ever read them when they come? — Russian novels and things I want to keep but not in our house in New Hope.

Dr. Tindall had left us knockout pills to calm Pip. Hypothetically, Pip would be sound asleep two hours after the pills were given.

Since we already knew the ins and outs of giving a cat a pill — you put it in, he spits it out — we were wary.

We resorted to silly talk, hoping that we'd catch Pip off-guard. "Take your medicine like a good ol' boy," Bob said. A bad Texas accent didn't fool Pip.

Finally, I used our foolproof method and ground the pills up in his food. Pip had favorites, although they changed whenever I bought cases on sale. I don't know how he knew, but invariably he turned up his nose at anything I bought at a discount.

Pip obviously hadn't seen the cases of savory salmon in the cupboard, so he cooperated and ate. The way to undo a cat is through his stomach, delicate or not. We waited for Pip to fall asleep. Since he slept

most of the morning anyway it was difficult to determine the effect of the pill versus his natural state. He
curled up on the chair. I tiptoed in and out of the
room, checking on him.

The vet had warned us about the third eyelid, how
when a cat sleeps a protective membrane comes up
from the bottom of the eye. Otherwise, I would have
had Pip at the ophthalmologist long ago.

I picked him up from the cushion on the chair and
carried him to the car—so far so good. I put my ear
close to him to make certain he was breathing.

We decided a carrier would frighten him, so I put
him down on his bed and closed the car door. Instantly, wide-eyed, yowling, he was awake. He reminded me of the cartoons where you see a cat's tail
plugged into an outlet.

Only temporarily, we thought. After all, these were
knockout pills. We tried telling him how lucky he was
because most cats ride in small containers, and he had
a whole station wagon to himself with two chauffeurs
at his beck and call.

Bob tried to reassure him. He even sang a lullaby.
We had treats and milk and a goose-down pillow and
a vocalist. "Anything you want," Bob said. What Pip
wanted was to get out and have Bob stop singing.

Pip yowled and caterwauled in unison with Bob.
He hung from the roof of the car upside down. He
managed to stay that way for the first ten miles, defying
gravity. Finally he discovered he could make louder,
more pitiful sounds if he stood on the back of the front

seat and screeched into our ears. When the man at the turnpike entrance handed us our ticket and said, "Have a good day," we could hardly hear him. We were going deaf from the noise.

Pip meanwhile set up camp in the back on top of a dried flower arrangement I had made especially for the dining room table.

By mile one-hundred he had calmed down a little, and set off to explore everything in the car, including the driver. He preferred the view from the brake pedal. It was one of the rare times he seemed to enjoy looking up, instead of down at us.

He stopped crooning by mile two-hundred. I no longer saw any trace of the third eyelid. He was awake and had started to use the back of the car as a race track. He shunned his bed and sat on top of his scratching post, assuming a loftier, more natural position.

We thought he was relaxing. He was getting his second wind.

We stopped for gas at an out-of-the-way station in upstate New York. The sign off of I-81 seemed simple enough — Gas This Way. By the time we got to Al's Service I was certain we would see bilingual signs welcoming us to Canada.

It was time to walk Pip. We had read a book on traveling with a cat. Obviously, it was ghostwritten. It was, as they say, a book that will live in infamy in the annals of bad advice.

"It is helpful to walk your animal when you stop

for gas. This will give them needed exercise and make them happy for the rest of the trip."

I took out the leash and hooked it to Pip's collar. I started off toward the bushes with Al staring at me. At first I thought it was because he valued his landscaping and did not want anything dropped beneath his brambles.

I assured him with my eyes, and the help of a leaping cat, that I had no intention, and neither did Pip, of soiling his property. Pip was interested in the woods.

Pip trotted along, going under the prickly wild roses, and dragging me through them. He was out for revenge and had no intention of going back to the car.

Finally, I gave the leash a tug. Pip sat down and moved backwards. It was then I realized he was trying to be Houdini and get out of his collar. I scooped him up and hurried back to the car.

"Don't see that much," Al said.

I nodded.

"Walking a cat, I mean. Don't see that at all."

"He's trained," I said.

"I can see that." He looked at the burrs on my pant legs.

Pip was miffed. I unsnapped the leash, and put him in the back on his favorite box, which he now decided he hated. He stomped across my dried flower arrangement again and stared out the window as we drove away toward the border.

When we changed drivers, Pip changed his tactics from sullenness to an all-out attack. He slunk across the front seat and jumped on the floor.

Scratch! Scratch! He pulled his claws back and forth across the green carpet. Perhaps had we told him we hated its ugly color and didn't care, he might have stopped. Instead we ignored him. My mother always said that children did not like to play to an empty theater.

We soon found out that ignoring Pip worked to his advantage, not ours. Like the most practiced of abusers, he was out to leave a mark where it didn't show. He sat on my lap, purring, and began to use my jeans as a scratching post.

By the time we reached the border he was asleep.

"We're in Canada now. Look at the water. The Thousand Islands." Pip detested water in almost any form except the toilet bowl, and didn't open an eye. I kept remembering our family trips to Canada. After we had been driving an hour, my sisters and I would say, "Are we in Canada yet, Dad?" Pip's lack of enthusiasm for anything other than destruction should have forewarned us.

I had all the health documents in my hand. I pushed the button for my window and by mistake hit the large rear window.

"Where are you folks from?" the customs man asked.

"Pennsylvania," I answered as Bob said, "New

York." We seemed to be just your average, estranged couple. "The States," we said, looking at each other. At least we agreed on that.

"Any building materials? Nails?"

We shook our heads. It was one of the few things that we weren't bringing into Canada.

"We have a cat," I said, and I handed him Pip's vaccination certificate, a sort of cat passport. The paper stated that Pip was a DSH (domestic shorthair, not a member of a Big Eight accounting firm), and that he had been vaccinated against everything except measles and car sickness.

"Where's the cat?" the man said.

I pointed to the back. No Pip. I pointed again.

He looked at me as if I were James Stewart traveling with a large, white, invisible rabbit. He handed me back the papers and told us that he hoped we found our cat.

"We've lost him," I said to Bob. "We've lost Pip."

"How can we lose a cat in a car? He's under something. He couldn't get out."

Then we remembered the open window.

I stopped the car and pulled over to the side where they examined the cars. I was prepared to unload everything. They'd see curtain rods and a case of wine and an electric grill—all contraband. But we hadn't lied. We truly didn't have any building materials.

Dr. Tindall had said that cats used a magnetic field to determine direction. Until they reorient themselves they could get lost. If Pip had escaped, he would be on his way back to Pennsylvania.

Just as I was about to rip the car apart, Pip resurfaced. He had been sleeping in a box filled with our lunch. This seemed to remind him he was hungry. I hadn't intended to feed him in the car. Having checked with the vet, I was certain Pip could survive nine hours without food. Bob and I couldn't.

Though ham was not Pip's favorite, he gave every indication that he would consider taking a bite. He jumped on my lap and put his paws against my chest and licked part of my sandwich. I remember when I was growing up and there was only one piece of pie left, my sister Ann would wet her fork with her tongue and put it on the pie, declaring the dessert hers.

Pip used a slightly modified, but effective technique. I relinquished my sandwich to him more easily than he would have given up his Fancy Feast. He bit into the sandwich and spit it out—a culinary snob, not content with the simple things in life. Disgruntled, he went back to ransacking the car.

Though I was pretty sure he could not read, he sat on everything I had marked Fragile. With a great flourish and a leap, he pounced on a box of crystal. He finally tired of somersaulting at mile 450. The last fifty miles we wondered how we were going to get him out of the car and into the house without him fleeing. We were determined to foil any escape plans.

"Do you hear that scratching?" Bob said. "It sounds as if he's digging."

As I turned around, two dried hydrangeas flew into the air. "I don't hear anything," I said, ignoring the sounds. I looked for Pip, who seemed to be hiding.

It was getting dark, and we knew that cats see better in the dark than we do. I kept hearing Dr. Tindall tell us to grab him by the scruff of the neck the way mother cats do. I have always wanted to tell Tindall that mother cats grab their babies with their teeth.

The scratching increased as we pulled off the main highway and onto a dirt road. It sounded as if Pip were trying to tunnel his way out before we reached the house.

When I was a child, my sisters and I used to fight over who would open the gate leading down to our house. Now there is only one post standing with a rusty hinge embedded in the wood. A long time ago our neighbor had cattle and horses, and if the gate was left open, we would find his farm in our backyard. Though we rigorously denied doing it, my sisters and I sometimes left the gate open.

Our parents wanted us to see nature up close — raccoons prying the lids off garbage cans, porcupines whittling the wood on our porch — but cows eating our grass were shooed away.

"Raccoons," I said to Bob. "There are raccoons up here."

"We have raccoons at home."

"But these are smarter, meaner," I said, remembering one surly raccoon that wanted a better grade of garbage. "If Pip gets loose and he meets a Canadian raccoon . . ."

"We could stay in the car for two weeks," Bob said.

Pip began to yowl as we turned into the driveway.

We decided that I would grab him and rush him into the house. Bob would hold open the door, an integral part of the plan.

"We have to be quick," Bob said, fumbling with the car door. "Everything's going to be fine."

I was not reassured. I was certain someone had said the same thing to Joan of Arc.

I grabbed Pip and headed for the door. I was reminded of that old story of what was behind the door, the lady or the tiger. What I could definitely say was that it was not Bob. He was at a different door. Screaming does not soothe a squirming cat, so I mildly yelled to Bob and asked him where he was. He finally opened the right door. Pip jumped down, took a swipe at my leg, and fled underneath the kitchen table to sulk.

I did not like the look on his face. He put his paws beneath his chin, elevating his glare. We knew it was only a matter of time before he exacted his revenge, but for now he would wait. Tomorrow was another day, and he had to get his sleep in order to outwit us.

CHAPTER 8

LANDED IMMIGRANT

*I*t was only five o'clock in the morning and Pip was chirping as he did his calisthenics on our bedroom rug. "Bad cat. Rotten cat," I said, using more adjectives than usual to show my disapproval. He moved closer to our beds and scratched furiously, just in case our hearing was failing.

"Bad cat," I said again, just in case *his* hearing was failing.

It was too early to explain to him the customs of the country. "This is not the United States," I started to say. I was beginning to sound as if I were either a guide asking my group to behave and not act like ugly Americans, or an officer sending a squad of raw recruits off into the jungle. Pip was too busy trying to reweave our rug to listen.

I realized it was pointless. As Bob often said, we were afternoon people, and I wasn't about to be taken advantage of so early on in Canada. Pip would have to wait to be told the rules, preferably in a room without a carpet.

99

Dr. Tindall had warned us about letting Pip outside too soon. We knew that we had three more days of housebound Mr. Obnoxious and that he was only warming up. We thought of giving him a compass and tying a note around his neck like Paddington Bear—if this cat is lost, please take him to darkest Kaminiskeg Lake. We weren't certain we wanted to be more specific about the address.

Pip was on a dusting binge, moving across the tops of furniture and sweeping them with his tail, knocking things off. We finally decided there was nothing else to do except eat breakfast. Pip agreed with our suggestion. The cat food, which he loved in New Hope, he hated in Canada. He probably wanted trout and black bass. He settled for eggs, my eggs, and then huffed off.

By mid-morning, when we were about ready to go into town for groceries, Pip discovered the archway of white birch in the dining room. He climbed up one side and hung from the cross pieces at the top. When we came in he was swinging. I rescued him by getting a stepladder. He looked grateful for all of a few seconds, and when I left, he climbed back up and assumed the same acrobatic pose.

Our neighbor, Fred, knocked on the door and came in just as Bob was rescuing Pip. He dispensed with the usual greeting and handed us a jar of blackberry jam his mother had made.

"Hear you got a cat," he said.

As far as we knew, cats were still legal in Canada.

From Pip's point of view, looking down on Nellie was the natural order of things.

He looked serious. "Lot of foxes," he said. "Those lads are bold."

"Foxes eat mice and squirrels," I said.

He stared at me and nodded. "And cats."

"Cats?"

"Well, they could if they wanted to." And then as an afterthought he told me not to worry. "I've only lost one cat."

"To a fox?"

He shook his head. End of conversation. I was just as glad. Next he would probably tell me about timber wolves bringing down a herd of deer in his field.

"There's a black bear with cubs by the garbage dump. Surprised me one day. If you can't outrun 'em, and you can't, climb a tree too small for it to climb."

"Is that what you did?" Bob said. Our neighbor is husky, wide-hipped, and long-legged.

He told us he laid on the ground and pretended to be dead. As he started to leave, he looked up at Pip on the archway. "I remember when your grandmother wanted to hang something from that archway, and your granddad, he said, 'No. Nothing hangs from that birch.' Nothing," he repeated, staring at Pip. "Mom put too much sugar in the jam," he said.

"Bears. Foxes. Anything else?" I asked.

"You remember old Barney? A rabid squirrel bit him."

All at once the enchanted forest was turning into a Grimm's fairy tale. I began to think that if we ever let Pip outside he would have to carry a gun.

Bob was more realistic. Our neighbor had pets, three dogs and a cat, and they survived. "Besides," he said, "have you ever seen a fox in *all* your years up here?"

"Once," I recalled. I was three and in Algonquin Park sitting on a log and eating a piece of chocolate cake, when a little red fox came up and took a bite off my cake. I took another bite. It did the same.

Rabies was prevalent then, and my parents, trained in the Old Yeller school of misinformation, thought you could get rabies only from the bite of an animal, and not its saliva.

"See," Bob said, triumphantly. "Look how long ago that was."

I finally decided the only sensible thing to do was to keep Pip inside. Unless the animals were into breaking and entering, he would be safe. Bob, always practical, said that we would have to replace not only the carpets, but the archway as well.

We left Pip to sulk and explore the house while we went to town. I weakened in the grocery store and bought Pip a can of tunafish on sale. I figured I would use it in our negotiations.

Pip was waiting for us at the door. In fact he was waiting for us on the screen door. He was already discovering things to do that he had never done before. While our friends who owned cats talked about the destruction of their screen doors, we said that Pip respected property. After we removed his claws from the door, he hiked off to project number two—rearranging the curtains.

In the evening he seemed intent on helping us carry in the wood, or at least undermining our efforts. For someone who had never carried anything heavier than a mouse, he stood at the door waiting to assist.

When we ate dinner, he joined us at the table. We ignored him until he tried to stand in the mashed potatoes.

Day two we decided that we would walk Pip and show him the property. I put the leash on him and told him our game plan. He seemed pleased, and paid as much attention as he could muster. Off we went, the three of us out the back door onto a small landing with steps. Pip decided to take the lead both literally and figuratively. He jumped down the steps, while I stumbled behind. At the bottom of the steps was a chipmunk. The chipmunk saw Pip and the thing he was dragging behind, and both of them took off. I had both Pip's collar and the leash in my hand, but no Pip.

I figured he was on his way to Toronto, but he raced underneath the house through an opening in the latticework. The house is set on concrete blocks to allow melting snow to run off into the lake without taking the house with it.

When I was a child, my cousins and I would play spies underneath the house. I remember thinking how much fun that was, but now the idea of crawling on my hands and knees to catch a cat that was trying to catch a chipmunk seemed rather silly.

Bob, who was decidedly more agile, said I knew the terrain better. I made a note to stop telling him my childhood stories. Every time I came close enough to Pip to grab him, he moved. Even though Pip and I were both on all fours, he was considerably more adept at maneuvering among the concrete blocks. Finally I grabbed Pip by the back legs, and handed him to Bob, who assisted me with a can of treats. Even the chipmunk was amazed.

Once Pip was safely inside we decided that walking a cat was for the birds. While I wiped the dirt off my face and hands, Pip distanced himself from me. He was still a white cat. No dirt. No mud. Forced exercise did nothing to improve his disposition.

Day three, we let Pip out.

We tried to encourage him to find his own space, preferably one not near us. The first problem he encountered were the chipmunks. Except for his brief encounter with one under the house, he had never seen a chipmunk before. Chipmunks are rodents, and Pip recognized this immediately. He knew a mouse even if it was disguised with stripes.

Therefore, he did not alter his method of attack — the long, slow kill. He waited patiently while the chipmunk gathered nuts and berries, and then he made a run for it. Only the chipmunk was faster, and Pip couldn't figure out where it went. Eventually he realized that this mouse climbed trees.

It lived in a hollow in a large red-pine tree. By now Pip had revised his original strategy. He camouflaged himself by standing near a birch tree.

Before Pip came into our lives, Bob and I left peanuts on the porch for the chipmunks, following our family tradition. My father even named the chipmunks he fed. By the end of summer, they would come up and eat the nuts from his hands. He called them all Alvin regardless of sex. Their surnames were numbers in ascending order. I had problems that Pip was stalking Alvin I's progeny.

One day Pip made his move. The chipmunk had dropped an acorn, and was in the process of retrieving it when Pip jumped. I watched both of them race across the lawn, heading for the giant red pine.

I knew Pip could not scale a tree whose branches started twenty feet up. I was wrong. Up the two of them went, Pip propelled by sheer will. He should have had cleats on his paws. The more the chipmunk squeaked and teased him, the higher Pip climbed.

I waited for him to come down, and after a while I heard a cry. Now Pip had several different sounds, and this was his "Help me." He was stuck out on a branch. I tried to coax him down part way. I'd seen enough bad movies to play the part of either a person of the cloth or a cop.

I thought of getting a rope, and a lot of sillier things. Eventually, I got the car. I put a blanket on the hood, then stood on it with another blanket in my arms and told Pip to jump. He probably thought this movie mania had gone too far, but after thirty minutes he jumped. The ingrate leapt from my arms onto the hood and onto the ground without so much as a meow.

The flora and fauna of Canada amazed Pip. He was not into botany in any way except for a few house plants he tormented and whose lives he shortened. Always immaculate, with white fur gleaming, he was not getting sticky. I tried telling him it was from the pine trees, and that he was a sap to use them as scratching posts. As usual, he disregarded my advice. He groomed furiously, and often I would see him with a tiny beard on his tongue.

Pip working out on the porch in Canada.

Pip settled into a routine. Mornings were spent licking pitch from his fur and trying to kill the chipmunk. In the afternoons he went to the beach to sun himself and use his giant litter box. Tiring of work, he then slept until it was time to eat.

I decided one day to give him a treat of a can of tunafish that Bob was planning to eat for lunch. "It's for Pip," I said. I told him that I had bought it for Pip as a reward for being a good boy. Bob reminded me of our nights in front of the fireplace and reached for a loaf of bread. As Bob opened the wrapper, Pip jumped onto the counter. He seemed to like the idea of breaking bread together, and he pushed the tuna can with his paw, toward him and away from Bob.

Pip would have preferred the whole fish, but the smell finally won him over. I filled his dish, and he did his part by gobbling up the food quickly. Pip came over to me and rubbed up against me, purring sweetly. When I looked as if I was considering not giving him any more, he increased his purring. I held out, trying to erase my image as an easy mark. He rubbed up against me.

I still think, despite what the experts say, that Pip was not marking territory. He was showing how much he loved us, how much he appreciated my taste in clothes, and the quality of the tuna.

Pip finished his tuna and started to beg. He did everything but carry his empty bowl in his mouth. I think he tried until he discovered how heavy it was.

I told him firmly that enough was enough, and as I started to tell him about starving cats, he turned tail and ran.

The next morning he was still asleep on a bed in the back room. My sisters and their friends used to sleep there. I was the outsider, the runt, the pest. I still cannot go in that room without hearing voices telling me to get out.

I looked in on Pip. He was curled up. He tried to raise his head when he saw me, but he put it down. He had thrown up.

I am a hoverer by nature. As Mother would say, I

didn't get it from the neighbors. When my sisters and I were sick, she would wipe our foreheads with a wet towel and sit with us. Everything that Mother did when we were children—reading *Little Women*, *Winnie-the-Pooh*, even Dickens, whom she loathed—seemed inappropriate with Pip.

I stroked Pip's head. With all the fur I couldn't tell if he was warm. I called our neighbor to ask him to recommend a vet.

"Is there one in town?" I asked.

"Do you like your cat?"

"Of course I like my cat."

"Then don't take him there. Go to Renfrew," he said.

Renfrew was sixty miles away. I called Dr. Tindall instead, who admitted that this was the first time he had treated a patient in Canada by phone.

I told him that I had given Pip a can of tunafish.

"Probably an upset stomach. Take his temperature, and if he has a fever . . ."

I was reeling. "Take his temperature?" I thought about putting a thermometer in Pip's mouth and holding it shut, but Tindall soon set me straight.

Pip was as receptive to having his temperature taken as he was to going for a midnight swim. Before I inserted the thermometer, he looked at me with sad eyes, and a stare that said, "I'll get you for this."

Pip had a fever. A cat's temperature is about two degrees higher than a human's. I called Dr. Tindall back. It seemed Pip had food poisoning. "Give him ampicillin.

Water. No food, and . . ." I knew he was going to say Pepto-Bismol.

I called the pharmacist. Her brother was a doctor, and she told me to call him and explain the situation.

"My cat," I said, stumbling over the words. "He needs liquid ampicillin." I felt as if I had been shoved onto a stage and asked to tap-dance. "Hit it, Sally!"

I started again. The doctor knew my family, and he was probably wondering when I had lost my mind. "My cat is sick. Temperature of 103."

"Okay," he said. I spelled Tindall for him. "Odd name," he said. His name was Chapeskie.

I drove up to the pharmacy, and on the bottle of ampicillin was "Sally Huxley cat." The medicine was pink. At least it wouldn't clash with the pink spots on Pip's fur from the aborted attempts to give him Pepto-Bismol.

Bob and I figured that a sick cat couldn't muster up enough energy to fight us off. Pip probably reasoned that if it were something I had given him to eat that made him sick he wasn't taking anything else without a food taster. He looked up, then curled into a ball again, covering his mouth with his paws. He wasn't taking any chances.

Finally I picked him up and held him, while Bob tipped his head back and squirted the stuff in his mouth. I find it hard to believe that Bob, a man with reasonably good eyesight, who can win a prize at a carnival for throwing a small ball into a ring floating in water, could mistake my dark hair for Pip's white fur. Pink is not my best color, especially when it is in my hair.

After two more attempts, we finally decided to squirt it on Pip's face around his mouth. Even when he was sick, Pip was a stickler about the way he looked. He groomed himself into good health.

Cats hide when they are sick. They do not like coddling or fussing, and resent someone hovering over them. I left Pip alone in peace for the rest of the day.

Bob maintained that he and Pip had similar habits when they were sick, but I never once heard Pip call out for orange juice, or ask to have his pillow fluffed, or remind me that a cold could be fatal.

That next afternoon I read in the newspaper about the scandal in the Canadian Ministry of Fishing — spoiled tuna that should have been dumped and not sold was put into some cat food and generic cans of tuna.

The headlines called it "The Caper Of The Tainted Cat Food." I couldn't tell Pip what had caused his sickness. I couldn't tell him that I had bought generic tuna on sale.

"Buy cheap, get cheap," my shoe repairman once told me when he refused to fix a pair of "worthless" sandals.

"Buy cheap, get cheap." With the phone calls, the medicine, a new thermometer, it was a high-priced brand of tuna after all.

We both learned a lesson, and Pip looked exceedingly smug for the next few days.

CHAPTER 9

BATCAT AND ROBERT

"*W*e have bats," I yelled to Bob. He was too intent on grilling steaks in the breezeway to see the squadron heading toward him. He is a purist, a charcoal man, and he was squirting water on the coals to keep the flames low. "Aim higher," I said, pointing at the bats coming from the attic.

The bats flew through the breezeway and then out into the open, gaining momentum. One bat turned toward Bob, who spread his arms and said, "Good eve—ning." Somehow I was not prepared to deal with Count Dracula at the grill.

"Don't encourage them," I said. "They're squatters. I want them to leave. Go back to their caves."

"Bats eat pests."

"Bats are pests," I said. "They carry rabies."

"We don't have to worry. They're nocturnal. We're never up that late anyway. We're afternoonal."

He was right, of course. The nocturnal member of our trio was taking a nap.

"Didn't you listen to Fred?" I said. Just this

morning our neighbor had been regaling us with stories of life in the wild with deranged animals.

Our house is set in the woods, surrounded by a
horseshoe of evergreens and birch, and according to
Fred, animals frothing at the mouth.

"Remember what Fred told us about rabid animals
howling in the night when they're near death?"

"Bats don't howl. They are very quiet. Besides, he
said that the bats were healthy in this part of Ontario."

Although I was not looking for their extinction, I
was disappointed to hear that they were long-lived.

The next day I called an exterminator after I saw a
bat hanging in the corner of a back bedroom. I was
afraid that, like an umbrella, it would open up in the
house and bring bad luck. I dispensed with the usual
greetings. "I have bats," I said. "Bats."

"I hear that a lot," he said. "Have you tried throwing smoke bombs? Mothballs?"

"My aim isn't good enough for that."

"No. No," he said. "You leave them around. Bats
hate the smell and go elsewhere."

"Like inside the house?"

"Well, maybe," he said, trying to reassure me.

He told me he would come to the house for an
estimate. I hoped he wasn't charging per bat because
at last count we had forty-five. He said the only thing
that gets rid of them is DDT, but he added that it also
could get rid of us.

When he arrived he said we had bats. I hoped that

was not the extent of his expertise. He noticed Pip slinking around the corner—the man had a van similar to Dr. Tindall's. "Bats are high-altitude mice," he said, looking at Pip who was hiding behind me. "Is your cat a good mouser?"

I nodded. As if to illustrate my point, Pip leapt into the grass, came up with nothing, and then turned his back and groomed as if that was what he wanted to do all along.

"Might not be a good batter," he said. "That's what you need. A good batter."

I had visions of Pip on a baseball card with a season's average of .001.

The man advised us to line the attic with heavy plastic and then spray foam insulation on top. Bats didn't like plastic, it seemed, but since our bats were squatters anyway they probably wouldn't mind if their accommodations were being renovated.

Everyone had remedies to get rid of bats. Leave the lights on all night because they can't function in the daytime. Light confuses them and disrupts their navigational systems. I think that suggestion was made by the power company.

Someone else told us to leave Pip outside. Then we would have to worry about our cat in addition to the bats.

"Play music," Fred said. "Heavy metal. That noise you Americans like."

I could see it all now—just your typical summer cottage occupied by Americans. First we gave Canada acid rain and now loud blaring music with a perimeter etched in lights.

I set up some ground rules—Live and let live. After all, they were presumably healthy Canadian bats and who was I, a foreigner, to determine their fate? I was being philosophical. They were being rude and messy—vandals with their own type of white graffiti. They could have cared less. They seemed to find the holes in the ceiling and equate them with indoor plumbing.

The people who built the house seventy years ago had used new lumber about as green as they were in the building business, and there were spaces between the boards of the ceiling. I'm certain they decided that as long as a child could not fall through the spaces, then the planks were close enough.

The house was added to over the years, and while the boards got closer together, so did the bats. They had set up housekeeping in the attic, and from time to time—for a change of scenery, I suppose—they dropped in on the rooms at the back of the house.

My sisters slept in the dorm, as they called it, a long rectangular room with four beds, of which only two were occupied. I was down the hall from them, but entering their room was like going through a series of locks, and my sisters controlled the water level.

I remembered once when I was young being asked into their room. I was pleased until I found out the invitation came with an asterisk. There was a low-flying bat in the room, and they believed that bats attacked the person with the longest hair. I was to be sacrificed as soon as I untied the ribbon around my ponytail.

The bat, however was a nonbeliever and ignored my hair. He clung to the wall, wings folded around him. Finally someone opened the window and it flew out. At least my sisters were kind enough to let me make my exit through the door instead of the window.

Since my hair is still long, I did not want to retest their theory by staying outside. Pip is a shorthair, so I wasn't worried.

Pip's experience with bats was more limited than mine. He had only seen their facsimile hanging from the chandelier at Halloween time. The next few nights Pip watched the bats from inside the kitchen.

The bats exited from a hole about the size of a quarter underneath the eaves in the cedar shakes on the house. They flew out, then dipped in much the same way as my high-school boyfriend slow-danced, before they shot up over the clothes line. Pip quivered, wiggling his rear. He looked like a bombardier through the windowpanes of the kitchen, with eyes as big as goggles.

Pip seemed encouraged at first by the slowness of the bats, but he learned something about inertia. While he stood still, the bats gained speed and momentum.

Eventually Pip tired of his behind-the-scenes view and moved to the steps outside the kitchen. He crouched, and when the bats swooped down, he'd spring at them. He was too slow. Though he was a fine jumper, a leftie with a perfect forearm, he was still approaching them from too low a level. The ground sloped near the house, and the closer Pip moved toward the eaves, the farther away he was from the flight path. He tried to climb the cedar shakes, but it was somewhat like scaling an icy mountain in tennis shoes. Pip's claws were not strong enough to get through the layers of paint.

Night after night we watched The Mighty Casey, as the exterminator might have called Pip, strike out.

The bats seemed to be calling in reinforcements to deal with this intruder. I gave up trying to count them after they appeared to be aiming for us, trying to ruin my census. Close up, they looked like ugly flying mice with fangs.

Pip would sit and look up at the eaves, tightening his muscles and getting into a leaping mode. We didn't know how he knew when they were ready to drop down, but he was waiting with open paws.

Sometimes he would look at them go by and turn his head as if watching a tennis ball. Other times he would leap in the air with his paw extended and swipe at them. They would sometimes come from both directions and cross. I rooted for a mid-air collision with no fatalities.

Eventually, Bob decided to assist Pip in his endeavor by moving the picnic table closer to the house. Pip was indifferent. He looked at the table and did the cat version of a shrug. When Bob left, Pip jumped on the table.

I was skeptical, and certain that a picnic table would only give him a better look at the bats as he missed them. If Bob wanted to rearrange the yard furniture to amuse Pip, that was fine with me, although I wasn't certain how we were going to eat the trout Bob was grilling with a fish-loving cat as the centerpiece. As I moved the silverware, Pip leapt off the table and hit a bat in mid-air, knocking it off course. The bat was able to regain altitude and fly out of enemy territory, even though the enemy was still in pursuit.

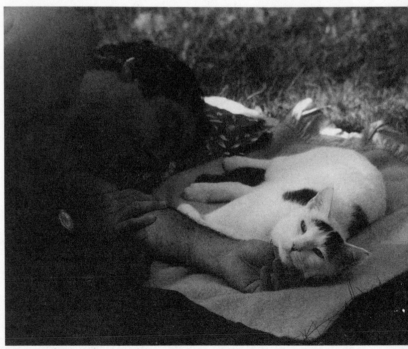

Batcat and Robert resting up in Canada before an evening of "batminton."

The next night I announced that the picnic table was not to be moved. I did not believe in blood sports.

"He isn't jumping at bunny rabbits," Bob said. "He's just having fun. Besides, you don't like bats."

"They eat pests," I said. I looked at Bob and smiled. "I heard that somewhere."

"You're the one who called an exterminator."

"That's different," I said. "It's not cruel and unusual punishment. Even our Supreme Court would disagree with your method."

Pip was poised on the table, which had already been moved. Bob seemed to be happy with his choice of a hit man, and patted him on the head.

The bats rested during the day. Something they had in common with Pip, although the resemblance stopped there. Bats hang upside down in caves or other dark places, and Pip's one effort was from the roof of the car.

One night we let Pip out at dusk for his usual evening stroll. We started calling him at nine to remind him of his curfew. No answer. We waited and called again. Then we called every five minutes. Neither of us could sleep. I was worried about the trap lines, which were over a mile away and not on our property, and Bob was worried that Pip had become disoriented and was lost. We plotted the route each of us would take the next morning to look for Pip. My map had all the scenic spots, such as the garbage dump and the brush pile.

When I realized I couldn't sleep, I moved to a

living-room chair and set up my command post. I tried to remember the first-aid course I had had in the eighth grade, but I had forgotten everything except artificial respiration and how I vowed never to put my lips on a boy's mouth.

Finally, at three o'clock when I called, Pip came swaggering through the woods. It was the cry he used when he had something in his mouth — a muted, yet bravado-filled meow.

I picked him up and hugged him. I told him how worried I was about him. He was nonplussed, although I suppose it was tough to be expressive with something hanging from his mouth. I made him drop it and went inside.

Bob praised him lavishly for coming back. He was Ulysses returning.

In the morning I went out to dispose of the mouse. It was crumpled with wings and fangs — clearly a bat. As the saying goes, it was a face only a mother could love, especially a mother with the same ugly face. Bob was proud of his pupil. "I taught him everything he knows about bats," Bob said to me. "You know they have the same navigational system as dolphins?"

I shook my head.

"Echolocation. Sort of like sonar."

I was beginning to wonder if I should organize a "Save the Bat" campaign.

Luckily, even though Batcat and Robert made a great team that summer, there was only one confirmed fatality.

CHAPTER *10*

CAT AND DOG

I had envisioned our life in the country as a feature story in Better Homes and Gardens, with Bob in the den, pipe in mouth, the ever faithful dog at his feet. I would be sitting on a chintz chair, discussing our drapes. Nowhere in this scene was there a cat sitting on a chair, *his* chair. After Pip moved in and took over our lives, we decided that we didn't need a dog even for a spread in a national magazine.

Bob had grown up with an English cocker who was called Biscuit because someone remarked that he was as cute as a "little biscuit." This revealed from the onset that we had differing ideas on the breed as well as the name of a dog. Rickey was my all-American cocker.

No doubt while Pip was on the road, he had formed lasting opinions about dogs. He feared them, and living with us had only reinforced his views. The rottweiler next door almost killed Pip in our garage.

In Canada, Pip had been frightened by Fred's hunting dogs. The morning we left we stopped at

Fred's house to say good-bye and were greeted by baying that conjured up images of misty moorlands and a skulking murderer. As we opened the door, Pip jumped from the car and fled through the bush.

Bob and I chased after him. I vowed to stay the winter if he couldn't find Pip. "I'll miss you," I said to my jogging companion, "but I have to stay with Pip."

Finally, just as we caught him, the dogs bayed again. Pip clawed me, and I let go, only to have Bob tell me that I should have held Pip tighter. Somehow the idea of spending a winter without Bob was gaining appeal.

Eventually, we trapped Pip and grabbed him by a back leg. As I held him, tightly this time, I could feel his heart beat. I never wanted him to be afraid of a dog again.

Dr. Tindall had warned us about getting an older dog, that the period of adjustment might be too much for Pip. With a puppy, Pip could establish his dominance from the beginning.

We didn't seriously consider getting a dog until my sister called and said that her dog's father had sired another litter. She wanted to give me a puppy for my birthday. I was noncommittal. There was a cat sitting on my lap at the time.

Bob finally decided that if we were ever to get a dog, now was the time. Besides, I was talking babies again, the type that weren't covered with fur.

Several months later my sister called again. Whoever said bad news travels fast was correct.

"Well, the puppies are here," she said.

I welcomed that news about as much as Paul Revere welcomed the sight of lanterns swinging. I tried to sound pleased. "Puppies," I said. I thought of all the times I had been forced to say something about a newborn. "What a nice head," or "Well, that's a baby," but sight unseen I had to improvise. There was a litter of nine, and if we wanted one . . . I was glad we didn't have to take them in multiples.

"Now you wanted a female?"

That was the one thing I could say with conviction. Brashly, we said we wanted the puppy. She was a southern belle, a springer spaniel born in Columbia, South Carolina, one of the cities burned by Sherman.

We talked to the owner of the sire, who raved about her and said that she could not be weaned until she was six weeks old. We could pick her up in South Carolina anytime after that.

I was not overjoyed about having a dog, probably because of the memories of my cocker spaniel. I remembered Rickey with fondness, waiting for me at the bus stop, actually hiding beneath the big spruce at the end of our driveway. He was not allowed up that far, but he would crawl on his stomach rather like a commando and inch his way under the white fence and then onto the grass across from the bus stop. I should have yelled at him, but I never did. I did not realize the danger of allowing a dog so close to the road. I wanted to remember my dog through the eyes of a child, when all the worries belonged to the adults.

It is difficult to keep a secret from cats. They make you spill the beans one way or another; even their staring takes on the look of an inquisitor. We figured the less Pip knew the better. Cats cannot spell, but I was certain that Pip understood us every time we said the word "dog." We began referring to the D-O-G as Nellie, named after Nell Gwyn.

We put off picking up Nellie as long as we could without appearing either ungrateful or unenthusiastic.

When we finally saw her, she was in a kennel with her mother, a long-nosed, handsome springer. Nellie had been bathed in the morning, but had found things to roll in that were best left unmentioned. She looked as if she were part pig.

"This is your new mommy," the kennel owner said as he handed me Nellie.

I pressed her close to me so I wouldn't have to look at her mashed-in face.

"Isn't she *beautiful?*"

"Now, that's a puppy," I said.

When I got back to the car with the bundle of black and white, I volunteered to drive. Graciously, Bob said he would take the first shift and smiled at the kennel owner, and then at me. I knew what he was thinking. I would have had to shove him out the door to drive. I had made a bed for Nellie in the back of our station wagon. I lifted her over the seat, out of view. "We did it," I said. Bob nodded, and I finally asked if he thought she was cute. "I mean aren't all puppies cute?"

*As a puppy Nellie had a face that only a mother
could love.*

"I thought so until now," he said.

Nellie began to cry, and I felt guilty, as if she
understood what I was saying. She tried to climb over
the seat, but her chubby tummy kept getting in the
way. I finally picked her up and held her in my lap.
She kept licking my hand. I patted her and looked at
her face. I was right. She wasn't a cute puppy. She
kept scratching her skin. I decided to be useful and
help her scratch—immediate bonding, whatever they
say.

I ruffled her fur and saw fleas. As we drove

through the Carolinas, I picked them off and threw them out the window. Even though fleas are biodegradable, the residents would probably think that I was just another Yankee ruining the landscape. By the end of the trip I felt itchy, and wanted to go to bed, but I knew our problems were just beginning. We had to face Pip.

I was hoping he had retired for the night. He was waiting for us in the kitchen, stretched out on the Brisker breadbox, keeping warm. We had been away three days, and despite being a cat he was glad to see us.

"How's our good boy?" we said, perhaps a little too effusively. He was already suspicious, and was hunkering down. His tail had moved into another gear.

Some animal psychologists theorize that when owners leave a cat for a longer period than usual the animal fears that a predator has eaten its owners, and goes into mourning. If that were true, Pip was already regretting his period of bereavement.

He dug his claws into the counter and focused on Nellie, who was running around on the floor, squeaking. He hung down, his eyes registering disbelief. He glared at Bob and me as only a cat can, and then he looked at Nellie again with such complete contempt that he denied her very existence. He jumped down and huffed off. He didn't stay around for proper introductions.

Dr. Tindall had told us stories about cats leaving home when their routine was disrupted. I thought of reinforcing his name tag, but I assured myself that he would never leave us.

Pip reappeared when we took Nellie down to the basement to go to sleep. He was probably entertaining ideas of a subterranean version of *Jane Eyre*. Perhaps Nellie, like Mrs. Rochester, would never emerge again. My grandfather's leather-bound copy of that book was Pip's favorite place to sit.

Pip took up guard duty at the top of the basement stairs.

We had cordoned off the middle room in the basement and blocked off the entrances with fire screens. Nellie had her bed, a stuffed lamb, and a radio with the station of our choice playing to keep her company. Despite the amenities, the basement with its cement floor, musty wooden beams, and pile of straw still looked like a Third World prison to me.

Pip did not like anything that in any way remotely resembled competition. The fact that Nellie had four feet and a tail was enough for him to dislike her instantly.

At night, after the news, Bob listened to classical music. The first night the Philadelphia Orchestra had an extra musician in our basement who whimpered and howled. Pip looked disgusted. Though he always slept through classical music, he seemed deeply offended that Nellie was ruining *Eine Kleine Nachtmusik* for him. He thumped down from his chair, landing on all four feet, and went to the basement door to hiss.

Nellie woke us all up early with her crying. We just lay in bed. Pip looked at us as if we should do something. Bob and I rolled over and put pillows over our heads, while Pip jumped from the bed and started down the back staircase.

We knew Pip was good-natured, kind, even-tempered, and he would never hurt Nellie. "Not to worry," we told each other, and then, as if we had both reached the same conclusion, we ran down the stairs after him.

He was sitting outside the room Nellie was in, staring at her through the fire screen, making faces. He raked his claws against the screen while she licked it from the other side.

Nellie was delighted. Since springers have cropped tails, they wag their entire body. She wiggled, got low to the ground, and turned in circles.

This annoyed Pip to no end—another hiss from him; nothing but adulation from her. We watched him from the staircase. He moved as close to the screen as he could, pressing his nose against it, giving him a thuggish look. Then he spit. Since spitting is against the law, even in New York subways, we told him to stop.

He seemed to resent the fact that we had chastised him in front of an "it," and slunk off in the direction of the laundry room, where he eventually put a hole in my detergent box with his claws. We feared this vandalism was only the beginning.

Nellie emerged from the basement noisy and dirty. We had left papers on the floor, but she preferred a dark corner, and then she rolled in it.

Pip was even more annoyed by the way she crunched her food. In a word, she was messy. More food was on the mat on the floor than in her mouth, and she pushed her dish around when she was finished. No self-respecting cat would ever appear to be that pleased with its food. She used her tongue, her mobile tongue, as we later called it, to clean the floor. She ate dust balls and cat hair and errant hardened peas with the same zest as her puppy food.

At first Pip tried intimidation, sneak attacks. He would lie in wait for her behind doors and underneath chairs. His plan was simple—hit and run to keep her on her toes and off him. He was quicker than she was. She was a jolly, lumbering little thing, who seemed to think she had found a friend. Dr. Tindall said we should not interfere and act as referees, that they had to reach their own accommodation. The only accommodation Pip probably had in mind was at another house.

By the end of the first week, Pip adopted a policy of benign neglect.

Nellie, on the other hand, pursued Pip with all the ardor of a suitor. She followed him as best she could. Pip learned how to walk around the kitchen without using the floor. We even moved his dining table to the counter, because Nellie tried to eat his food. Pip refused to even look at anything her tongue had touched.

If Nellie wanted to go down to the basement, which

Nellie was able to follow Pip in every direction
except up.

she rarely did without being forced to bed, Pip would brush by her and stop on the first step. Sometimes he would rub his nose against hers. Nellie quivered and cowered, boosting his ego.

We were worried that Pip might scratch Nellie's eyes. Nellie eventually learned to turn her head. A cat can hurt a dog's eyes, but as Tindall said, he never knew or heard of a cat killing a dog.

We watched Pip, his bravado being pushed to the limit. It was as if he were in one of those exercise studios where instructors urged, "Just one more push-up." We wanted to say, "Just one more swagger, Pip."

In time, each seemed to find comfort in having another animal around.

Nellie was destructive, something Pip had never been. As she ate her way through another chair leg, we began to think that she was a distant relative of a beaver. She was also into leather—my leather shoes. We moved the few intact kitchen chairs down to the basement for the duration of puppyhood.

By now Nellie had inveigled her way out of there and into a kitchen boudoir by hurling herself against the basement door and yowling as if she had broken every bone in her body. With equal determination and ingenuity she eventually found her permanent dwelling in the passageway between our bedroom and the sitting room.

Pip, whose position was firm on our bed, hissed at any further encroachment. Nellie was definitely ruining the neighorhood.

If Nellie crept close to the bed at night on one of her routine patrols, Pip would hang down from the bed and bat her. Her bed was a brown beanbag and his was a four-poster.

In the morning Pip would awaken first, making certain that he roused everyone. He would start down the stairs and then stop abruptly. Nellie, with her added weight, had the momentum, and often it was hard for her to stop and not pole-vault over Pip, who groomed and bided his time. It was just one of the small pleasures he had in his evolving relationship with her.

As Nellie started to grow up and become less rambunctious, Pip's attitude softened toward her. Her sudden movements had always unnerved him. I used to think when I looked at him as he was frightened by a squeaky toy or a wiggling body that he was remembering something from the past. I knew that it was only a reflex, but there was a part of Pip's life that I still wanted to know.

Nellie was spayed in Dr. Tindall's van, and as the anesthetic wore off, he carried her into our living room. I put a blanket for her in front of the fireplace to keep her warm. Pip played nurse. He lay down beside her, and licked her face.

I watched him from the doorway. Though I had long since realized that he would never hurt her, I wasn't certain what he would do. He never left her until she completely awakened and was able to stand. Afterwards, he ignored her again.

Later in the fall, Nellie became less and less of a

nuisance and more and more of a rival. If I patted one animal, Bob patted the other. There was a strong case of sibling rivalry. For the time being, they were the only children we had.

We began to take separate walks with Pip. It was the quality, not the quantity, but Pip wanted and needed both. He was so sensitive to the fact that Nellie was turning into something other than a pest, something substantial. She now weighed four times more than Pip, but he never abdicated his dominance. He used it sparingly, but he used it.

Pip had been an only child for so long that he probably just assumed it would always be that way. Animals are intuitive. They sense things that people cannot. I think our getting Nellie hurt him at first.

As spring turned to summer we began to plant a garden. Nellie was the chief digger. I had forgotten all the things that dogs do, but she was refreshing my memory.

Using her nose as if it were a divining rod, she sniffed the ground before she cultivated it with her front paws. She was even more helpful in planting bulbs, which she unearthed and then held in her jaws as she ran through the yard. I chased her around the yard three times with Pip in pursuit to get a hybrid lily from her mouth.

Pip always seemed to be in earshot when I scolded Nellie. He would sit, grooming, as I wrestled a bulb or a trowel from her and told her she was a "bad dog," something I assumed he thought was redundant.

Bob tried to plant his vegetable garden as usual, by

Like most older siblings, Pip inspired both fear and admiration in Nellie.

lining up a string before digging. He is so neat that he even wanted his vegetables in a straight row. Nellie rearranged his garden, and as the plants developed, she took shortcuts through them. Pip, of course, never disturbed a leaf.

Nellie was still a pest, a younger sister following after her brother. She sometimes sabotaged his hunting attempts. While he waited patiently at the edge of the field, Nellie rushed in as if she were his beater.

Pip was her mentor, and she watched and listened to him in a way she never did with us. She began to stretch the way Pip did, with one back leg up in the air, the other on the ground. Even her stares were complete cat. She could look at us in the same unflinching way, mustering up the best dog equivalent of contempt, and then at times, she remained pure dog, waiting to please, bringing us whatever slippers she hadn't eaten.

One day Nellie got her own mouse. It must have been lost and asking directions. Pip stopped searching through the dead grass and watched Nellie as she tried

Nellie did her best to entice Pip to play with her.

to emulate him by pouncing and poking at it. Then she tossed it up into the air and batted it.

Pip even brushed up against her while we deprived Nellie of her kill. We weren't taking any chances on what else she might do.

Often, from the window, I would watch them go off together, Pip leading, lifting his paws high, Nellie behind, sniffing, using her nose instead of her eyes to guide her. Pip would stop and look back to make certain she was following him.

Pip was the senior resident animal, the older brother. There were times when he ignored Nellie, when he hissed her away.

I was tempted to yell out, "Take your little sister along," but then I remembered the same words coming from my mother. I also remembered the words of my sisters, spoken quietly only to me, "If you come along, we won't bring you back."

CHAPTER 11

INSIDE OUT

A friend once described her cat as a spirit. One evening she watched as her calico sat in the yard, silent, his silhouette blurring in the dwindling light. Then, as if serendipity had struck, he leapt into the air. "It could have been a moth, a sudden breeze, even his shadow. I don't know," my friend said. "It was magical to watch him outside, dancing in the moonlight. The moment belonged to him."

When I asked her if she worried about allowing her pet outdoors, she told me that she loved him and she worried, but that she could not deny him his life as a cat.

Though domesticated, a cat retains some of its wildness, as if the years of breeding never completely tamed the animal, or altered its independent nature.

Dr. Tindall has called the cat the most adaptable of animals. "A cat's ability to survive on its own is so innate that man cannot override genetics by taking it into the house and pampering it."

Today the cat is the most popular domestic pet. Unlike the dog, the cat has a reputation of being able to care for itself and requires less human intrusion in its life. Dogs can easily be confined outdoors in a run or on a lead. It is simply not possible to restrain a cat in the same manner.

A new cat owner told me recently that her pet seemed to take care of himself. In the past, she and her husband had a dog that they kept tied in their yard.

"I let him out when he wants. He should be free. He's a cat." She looked at me earnestly, and then she said, "You should let a cat out, right?"

It wasn't an easy question to answer. Few would agree that an urban environment is the proper outdoor playground for a cat. But if the landscape changes and the sidewalks become yards, then there is an option of letting an inside cat outdoors part of the time.

The issue of whether a cat should be let outside provokes strong opinions. Those who believe that a cat should remain indoors at all times (the ins) are pragmatists, who argue that the animal is safer in the house, free from car accidents, dogs, wild animals, and other cats. They can point to statistics and facts to support their position. The outs have a different, perhaps romanticized view of a cat. They believe that somehow a cat is transformed when it is allowed beyond its four walls, that it only becomes a cat in the fresh air.

In the rural areas many cats were initially strays, and accustomed to being outside for at least part of their existence. After the animals have been reassured by food and shelter that they have found a new home, they seem to want to go outdoors.

There is also a sense that if a cat has survived on its own, it is aware of the dangers of outdoor living and should be allowed to come and go as it pleases. It is as if one somehow believes that each cat wears its own protective talisman to ward off danger and guarantee a minimum of nine lives.

A transplanted southerner lives in a large northeastern city with his two cats. He used to let them outside in Alabama. One cat is a Himalayan that now stares out the apartment window and tries to escape whenever a door is opened. "It's half a life for them here," he said. He knows that they miss running and scratching their noses on "that ole" rose bush. He feels that they were healthier outdoors, and he looks forward to all of them leaving the city.

Another proponent of the great outdoors is a retired antique dealer who runs an inn in Massachusetts.

"Do you believe I was thirty-nine before I had my first cat?"

That cat, a stray, walked into his shop and announced that she was here to stay by rubbing up against him and jumping on his desk. All that day, as he did his paperwork, he worked around her swishing tail.

"That was another century ago," he said, smiling. "Well, at least twenty cats ago."

He now has two dogs and two cats. He lets the cats out during the day, and brings them in at night. A white picket fence encloses his yard, but he knows cats can climb. The fence serves more as a lookout post than a deterrent. His cats seem to know they have a curfew, a bewitching hour in this New England town.

Tuesday, while not an army brat, has seen a lot of U.S. geography from the Plains states to New England to New York City.

"We got her on a Tuesday," Paula said. "Real inspired name. For a while she was a cat of a thousand nicknames but none stuck."

Long-legged, initially skinny, Tuesday would never be in contention for Miss Congeniality.

They allowed her out in Rhode Island. When they moved to New York City, Tuesday became a housebound cat, something she never liked. "She carried a memory of the outside with her," Paula said.

As part of a fitness routine and to placate the increasingly unhappy Tuesday, Paula and her husband tried to teach her to walk on a leash. Once they took her to Central Park. They were sitting on the grass reading with Tuesday between them when a dog raced by. As Tuesday took off, Paula launched herself and grabbed the end of the leash.

"If I hadn't," Paula said, "she'd have been in Hoboken."

When they were transferred to Kansas City, Tuesday was allowed out again. One time she returned with a cut from a wire or a fight with another cat.

"The vet was definitely one of those who cautioned against letting a cat out. He said too many things could happen. She could be in a fight, or run over, or lost, or stolen."

Paula was certain that no one would steal the unaffectionate Tuesday, but she thought about what the veterinarian had told her. "It didn't seem right to me to keep a cat in, when it had a chance to go out."

Even among veterinarians there is controversy about whether a cat should be let outside. Some suggest that housebound male cats who still spray, even though they are neutered, be allowed out for part of the time to curb their spraying indoors. Also, if a cat can claw a tree it may be less likely to savage a piece of furniture.

All veterinarians agree that an unneutered or unspayed cat should not be allowed outside. There are already too many unwanted stray cats.

There are risks in letting a cat outside. In rural areas where there is not much traffic there are problems associated with other animals. Dogs can kill cats. Usually, animals, such as a raccoon or a fox, will avoid contact with a cat. Outside of the domesticated animals, no animal, unless diseased, seems to kill without a reason.

Felines have a survival instinct, but most cat owners do not want to pit their animals against danger every day. Owners must be assured that the risks are outweighed by the cat's enjoyment.

Most shelters have an adoption policy that requires the owners to keep their cats indoors. The Bucks County SPCA is no exception. As I walked into the SPCA office, there was a three-legged cat on a ledge, purring and batting a paper clip. It rolled over so I could stroke its stomach. Its left front leg was withered and cut off above the knee.

The director looked at the cat and then at me. The cat, it seemed, was like a poster boy, an example of why an animal should not be allowed to roam. The cat was caught in a leghold trap. In parts of Pennsylvania, these traps are still legal.

"We have two like that," she said. The director is a soft-spoken woman. She motioned me inside her office, but it was clear that she would rather have stayed with the three-legged cat.

As I sat down, she looked at me, leveling her eyes, and shook her head. "One of the most discouraging things about letting a cat outside is that if it disappears, for whatever reason, you will never know what happened."

There are examples of a cat just moving on, leaving a home. For the most part, if a cat does not return, it's because it is dead or injured.

I know the litany by now. It is sensible, logical, and no one can disagree that there are more risks outside. However, it is also difficult to lay to rest the idea of a cat's independence, and its need to have an existence beyond four walls.

"We get the most calls about cats being hit by cars," she said. "Sometimes it is hard to avoid hitting a cat."

A cat will often sit at the side of a road and stare, and then, for no apparent reason, leap at a vehicle. Dr. Tindall thinks that it is because a cat only sees movement. A cat is at a greater risk at night because of lack of visibility on the part of the driver, and because the cat may not be able to determine the size of the moving object.

"Cats being killed by cars are what the public sees," she continued, "but there are other things equally deadly." As if he were cued, the three-legged cat appeared at the office door. "Diseases. If your cat is healthy it may contract a disease from another cat. And now there is an additional risk of rabies."

Like many, she felt that if a cat had not been outside it was content to sit on a window ledge and look at grass and trees through a pane of glass. She realized, she said, that some cats were satisfied to lie on the terrace in the sun. "Once you have an animal, you can use common sense, but common sense is a quality we can't give you."

Many of the complaints the SPCA receives are about neighborhood pets that roam. Often people do not want another animal on their property.

"We get calls about a neighbor threatening

Pip undercover on our terrace.

someone's cat. There is nothing we can do," she said.

She explained that because people were still accustomed to seeing cats out on their own, they don't report finding a stray. Some owners don't look for a cat if it is gone only a day or two. "They think it's just being a cat, but the longer a cat is missing, the greater the chance of not reuniting it and its owners."

On a darker side, many children who grow up to be abusers start by torturing cats. Even though most reported cases of cruelty to animals are against dogs, cats seem to engender special brutality. Unfortunately, there are people such as the timid boy in Mishima's *The Sailor Who Fell from Grace with the Sea* who became a "real man" in his friends' eyes by killing a kitten.

The SPCA is aware of such treatment of cats. "You don't want to know what has happened to some of them," the director said. For that reason, the SPCA has a policy of not allowing black cats to be adopted near Halloween.

As she started to say something else, there were sounds in the outer office. "No," a voice said. "We don't want a cat. Don't like them. We want a big dog. A good watcher."

The director shook her head and lowered her voice. "People have a mistaken idea about cats. Someday cats will get the respect they deserve."

Both the ins and the outs maintain that their position is the best for the cat—the ins to protect it, and the outs to preserve what its owners see as the essence of a cat.

What people do agree on is that cats that go outdoors should be spayed and neutered, vaccinated, and not allowed to annoy others.

Bob and I fell in between the ins and the outs. We realize that there are problems, and to be truthful I would feel better if a cat stayed inside. We now would not let a cat outside at night, nor would we go away, even for an hour or two, without putting a cat indoors. We would restrict a cat's freedom in the winter months, because of the cold, and because of a scarcity of food for a potential predator.

It is as if Pip never gave us a choice. I have often watched him outside, his fur glistening in the light, still wet from grooming. As contented and affectionate as he was to be ours, he needed to go outside. The view on a chair or on a window ledge was never enough for him. Perhaps, had he never experienced such freedom, or chased a leaf falling from a tree, turning in the breeze, or done battle with a squirrel, indoor living might have been acceptable.

It is not a question of right and wrong. As they say in the boxing world, it is often a split decision.

CHAPTER 12

GOODNIGHT, SWEET PRINCE

*N*either Pip nor I was ever a football fan, but I at least had my eyes open during the 1989 Rose Bowl game. Pip slept on the chair in the den. Bob and I had kept him inside New Year's Eve, and he was annoyed. His revelry had been confined to rubbing up against us, scratching at the door to go outside, and finally curling up on my lap at the stroke of midnight. We were worried about celebrants racing up and down the roads and maybe down our long driveway and into our yard as they had accidentally done two years before.

When Pip finally roused himself after snoozing through all of daytime football, he went into the kitchen. I had purposefully left some lobster on my plate—a gift to him for the New Year. In truth, lobster was Pip's favorite food. The few times a year we had it, I pretended to be too full to finish and in need of some assistance. Pip never failed to help me. He would wait patiently while I dug the meat out of the claw, purring, jumping on the kitchen counter.

He was his most beautiful that night, with white fur glistening. I watched him eat, licking the bowl, something he ordinarily might have considered too doglike. I remember looking at him an especially long time. It is a memory fixed in my mind. If I had known I was looking at him for the last time, I would have stopped him from going outside. I would have kept him inside for the rest of his life, but he wanted to go outside, and it was warm. I patted him on the head and as always told him to be home early.

I called for him to come inside at the usual time. Sometimes he waited on the porch, or underneath the yews, but that night he seemed to be nowhere.

It was warm for January, no snow, not even a cold night wind. I went outside with a flashlight and walked down the road that led to the barn and the garage. I called his name and whistled. I waited for him to bound from the field, unrepentant that he had scared me. I half expected to find him silhouetted beneath his favorite chestnut tree, looking very much like the sleek Egyptian cats immortalized in bronze by the artisans of the pharaohs. He was in none of his usual haunts.

I couldn't sleep. Bob and I searched for Pip. Then I went outside four times, each time calling his name and pleading with him to come. I even woke Roy up in the carriage house, who thought perhaps there was a burglar with a flashlight. When I told him about Pip, he said, "You know him. He can take care of himself."

I had a sick feeling and was afraid for daybreak to come. Nellie was anxious to go outside, and when Pip did not run to meet her, then ignore her, I knew that something was terribly wrong.

I walked down our long driveway, looking into the fields on either side, calling his name. I could not focus on the end of the driveway where the newspaper is tossed. In a dream once I had seen Pip lying dead at the end. I slowed my pace.

I was relieved that he wasn't there, but as I looked across the road I saw him lying underneath our neighbor's mailbox. Ironically, the number on the box was 212, New York City's area code. These things stick in one's mind, the first thoughts. I had wished, once, that we had taken Pip into the city and let him sit on the window ledges and watch the lights going on in the skyscrapers.

I focused on the black tail that had told me of his moods, that swished sometimes even in slumber. Here was my sweet boy lying dead, a trickle of pinkish blood in the white fur near his mouth. He looked asleep, stretched out the full length of his body. I picked him up and took him across the road. I screamed for Bob. Although I knew he could not hear me, I need to have him with me. I thought about the times I had carried Pip in my arms, when he squirmed and tried to jump down. This time all I could feel was his cold hardness.

I put Pip on the grass beneath a pine tree and started to run down the driveway to look for Bob. Then I realized I could not leave Pip alone a minute longer. I cradled him, wondering what I was going to do without him. He had been a large part of my life at the house. He had become a child to me. I picked him up, arms outstretched, and started to run.

Bob saw me and held Nellie back. I put Pip down in the heather bed and Nellie licked his face. It was her way of saying good-bye. Bob's and my good-byes were harder.

I had envisioned what it would be like when Pip grew old, when he could no longer jump, when going upstairs would be impossible. I would never have let him go. I would have denied him the right to die as he had lived, independently, without intrusion. It was one of Dr. Tindall and my frequent arguments. It was also a decision I would never have to make.

When I was young, we had a pet cemetery in the woods in back of our house. My father buried our animals. My sisters and I made crosses and bound the sticks together with twine. Even as a youngster, I wanted the animals to remember me, so before my father put the last shovel of dirt on the grave, I placed a dime on it, part of my allowance. It was a family tradition, never leave home without a dime if you need to make a phone call.

I am older now, with both my parents dead. My mother could not make me feel better, or speak lovingly of our pet, or plan a celebratory dinner in remembrance. Bob and I needed our traditions, our own rite of passage.

Bob lowered the flag to half-mast. I got Pip's favorite blanket, and we put on the new collar we had gotten him for Christmas, black velvet with rhinestones. We affixed his nametag. We never really pos-

Pip waits to ambush mice coming down to the stream to drink.

sessed him in life, but in death he would always belong to us.

I held Pip while Bob dug the grave behind the stone wall that Pip had used as a lookout post to ambush mice on their way to drink from the small creek. I could not bear to have his grave within my sight, to see it from the window out of which I used to watch for him. Bob used both a pick and a shovel, and then clippers to cut the roots of a sycamore to dig deep enough to bury Pip. It seemed appropriate that roots had to be severed, because losing Pip was like losing a part of ourselves.

I kept thinking that I should celebrate his life with us, that I should be grateful for the years we had, but all I could think of was, Why did we let him out? Why didn't I look for him sooner?

Dr. Tindall told us Pip was killed instantly. From what we can determine, Pip was at the edge of our field, when someone threw a beer bottle from a passing car. Instead of jumping back into the brambles of the field, he leapt in front of another car that was following behind. I am grateful to the people for not leaving him on the road to be hit again.

Bob and I stood, looking down at the ground. Having lived quite well without a cat for years, it now seemed impossible to go on without one. I called a friend and told her what had happened to Pip. We both cried and agreed that Bob and I needed another cat. That evening we went to her house. She knew a young couple who had been feeding some strays, and they told her if they could trap the sweet one, they would bring him over. Straggly, wild Oliver the gray tiger came into our lives that night, spitting, hissing, afraid.

That night as Oliver lay curled up under our hutch table in the kitchen, unwilling to come out, I missed Pip more than ever. I called a friend in New York and told her about Pip and how I would always regret letting him go outside. "You know Pip," she said. "He would never hold that against you." And then she half-whispered and said, "Ask him."

I went down to his grave and sat on a nearby stump. I told Pip how sorry I was that I had failed him. I used to kiss him and tell him that I would never let any harm come to him. I had not been able to keep that promise.

I told Pip about the new cat and how I knew he would not like him. Pip left a legacy. He taught us to love cats, though he would not have been gracious to any of his successors. I once remember Pip chasing a tiny black stray up our apple tree. He seemed proud, protective of us and his property. I told Pip that he should remember his past and be nice to the cat in the tree. I picked him up and carried him inside, allowing the stray to come down eventually and run away. I was wrong, I thought. I didn't want Pip to remember that he was a cat with two lives. I wanted him only to remember us.

I looked at his grave, at the marker we had made, and the wreath we had fashioned from a Christmas tree branch. I had to tell Pip again that he started it all.